Emergence: The John Bax Story

By
Pat McGrath Avery

Foreword by
George K. Peck

Emergence: The John Bax Story

ISBN: 978-1-937958-02-2 (Hardcover)
978-1-937958-04-6 (E-Book)

LCCN:

Cover Photo: Tony Mercieca, Eastern Screech Owls
Layout and Design: Susan Schnelbach

Red Engine Press
Printed in the USA

John Bax

John in the field

From Those Who Knew John Bax

"John's legacy will be his breathtaking videos and an arrangement with the Cornell Lab of Ornithology means his films will be around for others to enjoy long after John is gone. His passion will outlive him." - "John Bax: A Passion for Birds" by Steve Sinclair, (Coastal Current Weekly, October 28, 2011)

"Watching John's documentaries were a source of pure inspiration. His skill, talent and patience were obvious in everything he captured. I wished that I had come to the US sooner, so perhaps then I may have had an opportunity to assist John in the making of those wonderful documentaries. - Sandesh Kadur, Wildlife Filmmaker/Photographer

"John was the Pied Piper of birders in the Rio Grande Valley." - Glen Hindman, Birder from Fun n Sun, Harlingen, TX

"John had an incredible ability to find birds." - Tony Mercieca, Professional Photographer

"John's graphic cinematography and video cameras did a fantastic job of bringing out the bird's colors plus their constant verbal interactions." - Lee Zieger, Businessman and Photographer

"John took me under his wing and taught me about nature, birds and their behavior. He was my mentor and encouraged my photography." - Seth Patterson, Professional Photographer, Gorgas Science Foundation

"John was truly a pioneer in nature cinematography." - Larry Lof, Executive Director, Gorgas Science Foundation

"He possesses an incredible intellect and instinct of the natural world that is extraordinary." - Tony Vezo, Professional Photographer, Author

"I consider it a privilege to have known and worked with John over the years. I don't know of anyone with a more patient, respectful and loving attitude toward the wildlife he filmed." - Bob Bocking, Cinematographer and Film Editor

"I think John Bax deserves the term "Bird Whisperer" more than anyone; he instinctively knew where and how to find those nests, but with him, it was ALWAYS about the birds; they came first!" - Madeleine Sandefur, Avid Birder

Note from a friend: "John, I have benefitted greatly from knowing you. You are one of the few people I know who gives so much more to society than others, who only take."

First Annual
RIO GRANDE VALLEY BIRDING FESTIVAL
Harlingen, Texas
November 3 - 6, 1994

TROPICAL BIRDS OF THE BORDER

PROGRAM

Table of Contents

Foreword 1

Acknowledgements 5

Author's Notes. 7

Book One: John Bax's Life. 9
- Introduction 11
- Chapter 1: Belgium. 13
- Chapter 2: War Reaches Belgium 19
- Chapter 3: The Good Years, 1955–1965. 27
- Chapter 4: New Opportunity 35
- Chapter 5: A Flood of Memories 43

Book Two: John's Filming Expeditions 45
- Author's Note. 47
- Chapter 6: John Spreads His Wings 49
- Chapter 7: The 1980s 61
- Chapter 8: The 1990s 87
- Chapter 9: Birds of a Feather. 99
- Chapter 10: More Lives than a Cat. 111

Book Three: Films 121
- Introduction 123
- Birds of the Arctic Tundra, 1984 125
- The Man Who Loved Birds, 1986. 126
- The Treasure of Madera Canyon: John Bax in Arizona, 1989 . . . 128
- Journey to Brazoria, 1990 130
- At a Bend in the Mexican River, 1992 133
- El Cielo: Forest in the Clouds, 1993. 134
- Treasures of the Rio Grande Delta, 1994. 136
- A Passion for Birds, 1996. 138
- John's DVD Series. 142

Appendices 145
- Appendix I: Filming Expeditions 1975–1997. 147
- Appendix II: Film List 149
- Appendix III: John Bax's Life List. 153
- Bibliography 165

Foreword

The receipt of some nest cards he submitted in 1978 to the Ontario Nest Records Scheme at the Royal Ontario Museum in Toronto, a program that I have organized since 1966, was my first introduction to John Bax. In the next six years while living in London, Ontario, he contributed a total of 300 Ontario nests on cards to this breeding bird monitoring program. Although I knew little of John Bax at that time, other than that he was a bird cinematographer, his detailed nest cards were certainly appreciated.

Later, during bird photographic trips to Texas, and while at the Laguna Atascosa National Wildlife Refuge in the Rio Grande Valley, I learned that John had moved to the 'Valley', and was engaged in the cinematography of birds there and elsewhere. Many birders and ornithologists regard the Lower Rio Grande Valley in Texas as the premier birding site in all of North America north of Mexico. Situated as it is on the Rio Grande River and the Gulf of Mexico at a subtropical latitude, it attracts numerous tropical vagrants and as well the multitude of trans-gulf migrants each year moving north to breed. In the region are two outstanding National Wildlife Refuges, Santa Ana NWR and John's favourite, the Laguna Atascosa NWR. It also contains several state parks with great birding opportunities, the Audubon Society Sabal Palm Sanctuary, and South Padre Island. Thus, it was here in this avian-rich area that John decided to make his final home.

On another photographic field trip to Texas in 1996, I took the liberty of contacting John for information he might have of the region's nesting birds. And, thus began an association, which, although limited by time and distance, became memorable and important to me. Without any previous personal contact, John's generosity and willingness to help were obvious. I quickly became aware that here was a kindred spirit as he showed me such Texas specialties as nesting Least Grebe, White-tailed Kite, Harris's Hawk, White-tailed Hawk, Crested Caracara, Common Ground-Dove, Red-crowned Parrot, Green Parakeet, and Ringed Kingfisher. He procured for me a permit and key to some off-limit areas in the wonderful Laguna Atascosa National Wildlife Refuge, which allowed me to use photographic blinds there. John also told me of a friend of his who had a Plain Chachalaca nesting in an overhead planter on his patio, where I was able to obtain egg photographs. Such kindness was a testament to John's generosity of spirit to share these things he loved and was even more remarkable in light of the fact that I was, at the time, a virtual stranger. It was on this trip that I met his charming Texas-born wife Alice, whom he had married four years earlier. She was a beloved and, I believe, a necessary steadying influence on someone as obsessed with birds as John surely was. Subsequent to this trip we maintained contact by correspondence.

Again in 1998, his remarkable nest-finding ability was apparent, as he showed me nesting Barn Owls, Lesser Nighthawk, Great Kiskadee, and another nest of White-tailed Hawk. He introduced me to his long-time friend Tony Mercieca, an extremely talented bird photographer from California who made annual trips to Texas over many years to photograph the local birds and, latterly, to visit John. Tony had set up a tower blind on a White-tailed Hawk nest, which I was invited to use, and the ensuing experience will never be forgotten, as a pair of these magnificent raptors brought prey to their nestlings. Trips in Laguna with John and Tony revealed a treasure-trove of birds to see and photograph and even let us photograph a very aggressive and protective female alligator guarding her newly hatched young.

Ten years elapsed before I again was with John, this time on a 2008 field trip to the 'Valley' accompanied by three close birding friends. As before, contacting John led to an immediate offer to show us birds and nests. We met him near Laguna Atascosa and were shown a nesting Common Pauraque with two newly hatched young, territorial Crested Caracaras, and another White-tailed Kite nest with the adult hovering beautifully over the nest before alighting. A day later at his home in Port Isabel we saw his feeders which attracted a great assortment of birds and small mammals. From there we followed him to nests of White-tailed Hawk, Harris's Hawk, and on South Padre Island, other nests of Wilson's Plover and American Oystercatcher – all a tribute to his superior ability to find active nests, and his penchant for sharing these things he loved with others.

Viewing a number of his many films and videos was a visual delight. These films led him from the Canadian arctic, and western Canada, south to Texas, Central America, islands in the Caribbean, and South America. The films were far more than just recordings of the birds and their habitats. They revealed an artistic eye, a knowledge of photographic techniques, and above all a desire and purpose to portray the behaviour of birds during nesting, and feeding, while occupying their specific habitats. The beauty and uniqueness of his subjects dominated in each of his films. We can only marvel at the hours and days searching for birds and nests, and then the many hours crouched in a blind in order to get some of the lovely images he achieved.

It must remain a mystery why some of us find ourselves saddled or burdened with the singular passion and obsession for birds that dominate our lives and occupy our minds an inordinate amount of the time. It does not appear to be inherited, as many of our parents and siblings do not evidence it, but when it inexplicably occurs, it fills the mind, motivates and drives the paths of one's life, and is the source of both joy, and pain and often frustration. One of the most famous and obsessed birders, Roger Tory Peterson, of whom it has been noted that his eyes would glaze over and his interest wane when the conversation moved away from birds, once proclaimed that 'birds are the most vivid expression of life'. And for those of us, blessed or cursed with this passion for birds, it needs no explanation. John Bax lived his life with this obsession and for him it was a gift that demanded no apology, and enabled him to give to others his view of the beauty and passion he felt for birds.

George K. Peck
Research Associate in Ornithology
Royal Ontario Museum, Toronto

Acknowledgements

When John and I started tugging apart his life one strand at a time, I had limited knowledge of birding but great appreciation for his talent.

I researched, interviewed, took notes, wrote and researched some more. I let each little strand of information float around in the recesses of my mind. I watched and re-watched many of his films. Whenever I needed to get in tune with John's story, I watched a film again. Each of them takes me to a place he's been and shows me beauty through his eyes and camera lens.

I realized I needed to call on the experts. Nature lovers and photographers share an openness that continually pleases me.

Thank you to Scarlet Colley, South Padre Island's dolphin and birding expert, and Cate Ball who was the manager at the South Padre Island Birding & Nature Center. I learned about birding, nature and John Bax from both of you.

Janet Randall and other members of the Bay Area Birding Group, thank you for welcoming me into your group and sharing your collective knowledge with me. Madeleine Sandefur, a member of the group, is active in several area nature organizations. She travels frequently, taking awesome pictures, which she freely shares. Thank you, Madeleine.

Thanks to all the birders who shared memories of John.

Seth Patterson, Tony Mercieca, Lee Zieger, Steve Sinclair, Sandesh Kadur and Bill Purcell, six nature photographers extraordinaire, thank you for sharing your memories of John and the adventures you've shared. Thanks to Larry Lof and Bob Bocking for your "working with John" stories.

This book would have never happened without the tireless support of Alice Bax, John's wife. Not only did she spend countless hours gathering and sharing information, articles, videos and photos, she was the driving force through which John reconnected with his family and shared his life with others. John's sons and daughters-in-law shared their memories and family stories.

Thanks to his Belgian friends; Mieke Leppens and Jan Sterckx, for sharing memories. Jan, thanks for translating John's list of birds from Belgium.

Thank you to Joni Montover and Griff Mangan of Paragraphs on Padre Blvd for their encouragement. The store carries a line of John's nature DVDs.

A special thank you to Nan Wisherd, publisher, author and avid birder, who offered to edit my manuscript.

As always, thank you to Joyce Faulkner who shares her eye for beauty in designing book covers. Thank you to Susan Schnelbach for her patience and her creative talent in layout design.

A special thank you to my husband, Everett Avery, for the many hours he spent scanning and organizing pictures and documents, accompanying me on interviews and research trips, and generally keeping me organized.

Author's Notes

In the winter of 2010 I volunteered at the South Padre Island Birding and Nature Center where I met John and Alice Bax. John told me he liked to film birds. As we talked I told them I wanted to find the parrots that reside in the Rio Grande Valley. He and Alice offered to take me to Brownsville to find and photograph parrots and green parakeets.

After they left the birding center, Cate Ball, birding center manager, told me that John was a well-known cinematographer and was scheduled to make a series of presentations. The center would also be selling his DVDs.

The more time I spent with John, the more he piqued my interest. John was a study in contrasts. I was struck by his incredible gift and his humility. Here was a man with an outstanding eye for beauty and yet his early years were haunted by the ugliness of poverty and war. As time went by, I realized that the man his friends and colleagues considered kind, humble and gifted was the same man his children remembered as strict, stoic and distant.

I thought of the many veterans I have interviewed, but I've never interviewed or written about a child growing up under Nazi occupation during WWII. After the war, many veterans wanted to forget and move forward. Society expected nothing less and troubled memories remained hidden. Many found it difficult to communicate with family, friends and co-workers. I wondered if children of war experienced the same difficulty in adjusting to ordinary life and relationships. PTSD (Post-Traumatic Stress Disorder) would not be recognized until years later.

Combine that with my budding interest in birding, and John captured my writer's imagination.

I searched every corner of my brain for a title that would reflect the dichotomy of John's life. In a brainstorming session, Joyce Faulkner and I talked about how his life was a process of emerging… Thus the title that captures John's journey!

* Spelling note: I have left John's and George Peck's spelling according to the "Queen's English" aka British English. You will notice words like "colour" and "behaviour." In American English, the spelling would be: "color" and "behavior." For more information on the differences, see http://en.wikipedia.org/wiki/American_and_British_English_spelling.

In respect to John's love of birds, I've chosen to capitalize the species names. It is accepted practice in birding and scientific circles to use them as proper nouns; in ordinary writing, it is correct to use the titles as common nouns.

Book One: John Bax's Life

Introduction

"John's search for beauty and nature has meant that much of his life has been spent in the field, camping out, living simply, carrying what he needed on his back." from A Passion for Birds *by Gorgas Science Foundation*

"Mosquitoes, not talking millions…billions and billions all the time." John remarked in the film about the Brazoria National Wildlife Refuge, a Texas coast habitat located south of Houston and north of Freeport. It is one of three national wildlife refuges – along with San Bernard and Big Boggy - that make up the Texas Mid-coast National Wildlife Refuge Complex.

Mosquitoes, flies, ice, hypothermia, heat, and months of seclusion: none of these mattered as long as John held a camera in hand and a bird in sight.

Imagine ten to twelve hours a day, day after day, week after week, and month after month, in a 4' × 4' blind with searing heat or extreme cold, bugs, snakes and absolute silence except for the sounds of nature.

John Bax spent a lifetime traipsing the rainforest, wandering through Canadian woodlands, camping in the Arctic tundra, Mexico and Central America, and visiting parks and wildlife preserves around the world. Carrying his camera and tripod, he followed the birds. He lived his passion.

"If you find their home and wait long enough, the birds will come." John's philosophy gave him patience.

He filmed the Snow Geese, Sandhill Cranes, dancing Western Grebes, the Bumblebee Hummingbirds, Mountain Trogons, and other rare and exotic species.

"Birds can't count," John laughed. "I tried to take someone into the blind with me. They would leave and the birds didn't know I was still there."

John's story takes him from Belgium to Canada, the United States, and throughout the Americas.

****

"Always hungry, afraid of my dad and looking for birds. Those are the strongest memories from my childhood," John told me.

"Do you remember when you first discovered birds?" I imagined John's early fascination.

"I always liked them, as long as I remember. There are incidents I remember, like our neighbors loaning me binoculars. Mostly I remember wanting to be in the woods looking for them.

"Our home wasn't a happy one so we stayed away as much as we could. Even before the war, things were bad." John grew silent with his memories.

"Was your life similar to your neighbors?" I wanted to get a feel for what Belgium was like in the 1930s and 1940s.

"In some ways. Nobody had cars or electricity. Most children I knew didn't have bicycles. You were either rich or poor and we were the poor. I don't think other children feared their dads like we did.

After the Germans came, fear became a way of life for everyone…the fear of the soldiers in the street, their guns…and later, the constant fear of the planes overhead."

John's life spanned the same era as my parents and the veterans I've written about. I had heard what life was like for American children. John's seemed far less desirable.

I found myself wondering if birds gave John a glimpse into a freedom he never knew. Maybe his soul hungered for beauty long before he understood why, or maybe God gave him an incredible gift that manifested itself even in the shambles that was John's childhood.

In any case, I wanted John to tell me more.

Chapter 1: Belgium

"Life wasn't easy in Belgium after WWI." John Bax

Like many of his generation, John's childhood years encompassed the grandeur of the "Old World" and the Nazi occupation of 20th-Century Europe.

Antwerp, located in northeastern Belgium, is the country's second largest city. (Brussels, the capital, is the largest.) Antwerp was a major European harbor, second only to Rotterdam. Before World War II, it was known for its 16th and 17th century architecture. Like much of Europe, it suffered devastation during the war.

Today, Antwerp is the eighth largest container port in the world.

John's story begins in the northeastern corner of Belgium in a small town called Turnhout. The town is located about seventeen miles northeast of Antwerp and about ten miles south of Holland.

Belgium is a small country about the size of Maryland. Today it has a population of ten million. Three national languages are spoken: Dutch or Flemish, French, and German. John's native language was Flemish.

Belgium has retained its old-world charm. Massive destruction occurred

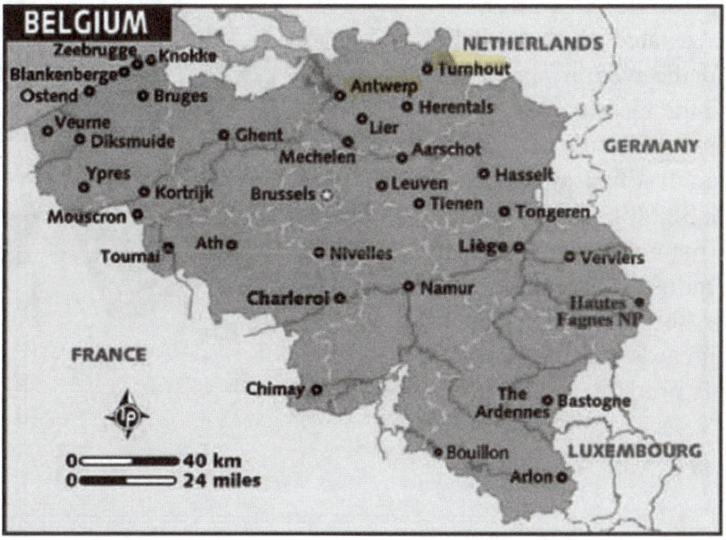

Map of Belgium

during World War II, but the country committed itself to the restoration and preservation of its historical buildings and traditions.

But long before that, Belgium suffered destruction. Its centuries-old history included major European wars. Because of its location, Belgium became a pawn of the Germans in World War I. Invaded at the beginning of the war it was the home of the infamous and bloody battle at Flanders Field.

At the end of WWI, Belgium lay in ruins. The 1920s and 1930s found the country rebuilding its political, economic and cultural structure. The street violence and citizen anger that had characterized the years following the war had mostly abated by the time of John's birth.

The economic woes of the average citizen had not. Even though John's dad had a job, the continual shortage of money controlled their lives.

"The average family didn't have electricity, telephones or cars. If families could afford it, they owned a horse-drawn carriage and, in some cases, a radio. Children didn't have bicycles. If and when we attended school, we walked," John said.

Children from poor and lower middle-class families attended grade school. If middle-class families could afford it, their children attended high school. The universities served only the rich.

Wealthy citizens owned the land in Belgium. A huge disparity existed between the lives of the wealthy landowners and the factory workers.

Turnhout, John's birthplace, is a small town of approximately 38,000. In the 1920s, paper manufacturing was its major industry. Already world-famous for its production of playing cards, the city boasted multiple production factories.

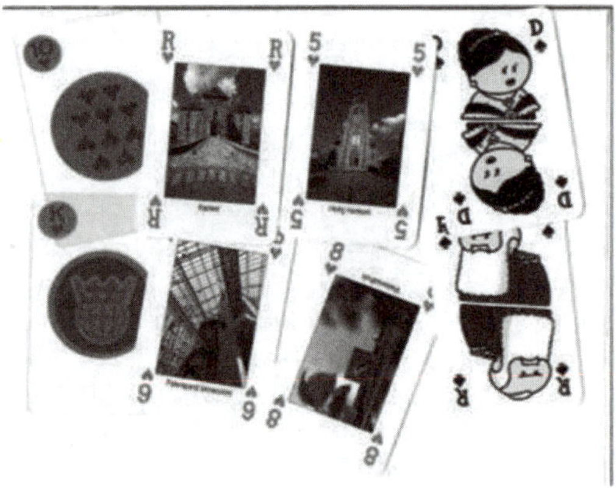

Sample playing card designs

John's Early Years

"Ever since I was a little boy in Belgium, I've liked to watch birds." John Bax

In 1925, Belgium, along with Germany, France, Great Britain and Italy, signed the Treaty of Mutual Guarantee (the Locarno Treaties) establishing the boundaries of their countries: "Germany and Belgium, and also Germany and France, mutually undertake that they will in no case attack or invade each other or resort to war against each other."

In 1925, Roman Catholics made up the majority of the Belgian population, huge numbers of Jews were immigrating to Belgium, the Socialist Party was gathering steam and political ideologies polarized people.

Fresh from prison in late 1924 and early 1925, Adolph Hitler reorganized his Nazi party. In a visit to Bavaria, he promised that the Nazi party would work within the rules of the democratic constitution.

Many people born in 1925 would rise to fame in the arts, including: Dick Van Dyke, Dina Merrill, Donald O'Connor, Flannery O'Connor, Hugh O'Brien, Fess Parker, Gore Vidal, Gwen Verdon, Hal Holbrook, Jimmy Dickens, Johnny Carson, Marty Robbins, Maureen Stapleton, Richard Burton, Rock Hudson and Sam Peckinpah. New York Yankee Baseball great Babe Ruth collapsed and was rushed to a hospital where he had surgery for an ulcer. (John loved movies. He loved movies and kept up on the life of his favorite stars.)

In 1925, Joseph Stalin served as General Secretary of the Central Committee in Russia, future British prime minister Margaret Thatcher was born, Field Marshall Paul von Hindenburg was elected president of Germany, Benito Mussolini dissolved Italy's parliament and became dictator, Canada House opened in London Ontario, and Calvin Coolidge became the first United States president to have his inauguration broadcast on radio. Walter Percy Chrysler founded The Chrysler Corporation and John Logie Baird created Britain's first television transmitter. Scotch tape, invented by 3M employee Richard G. Drew, became an overnight success. (John's son, Leo, would later work for, and retire from, 3M.)

The State vs. John T. Scopes (The Monkey Trial) brought the issue of teaching Darwin's theory of evolution to a courtroom in Tennessee, pitting William Jennings Bryan against Clarence Darrow in one of history's most famous trials. Al Capone took over the Chicago bootlegging racket. New York City surpassed London as the world's largest city.

In the United States, F. Scott Fitzgerald's *The Great Gatsby* was published. In Germany on July 18, the first volume of *Mein Kampf* by Adolph Hitler was published.

Seven days later, on July 25, 1925, Joannes (John) Bax came into this world, the son of a lower middle-class family. One can't help but wonder if the birds sang in anticipation of the man who would film, study, and befriend them.

****

John's dad worked in a metal factory. His mother was a housewife. Two younger brothers, Leo and Louie, came along in the following years.

Life at home was far from pleasant. John lived in fear of his father. "He was a womanizer…not a good family man," John remembered.

John's father was easily angered and quick with his hand. John learned to keep out of his way as much as possible. His mother did little to protect her children. Maybe she too had learned that the best tactic was to stay out of his way – or to ignore what she couldn't change. The society of the time required that she accept her lot in life.

However, John learned skills from his dad that would serve him well during the years of Nazi occupation. At an early age, John learned the arts of begging and poaching. His brothers, Leo and Louie, did not share in these experiences. John's adventurous nature fit into the survival mode of war's children. His family lived close to a wealthy land holding with an excess of wildlife. It proved easier to poach small animals from this abundance rather than stretch the family budget from dollars earned at the factory.

Begging worked too. It was easy to knock on the farmer's door and ask for food. From each farmer, John asked for only a few potatoes. By the end of the day, John acquired plenty of food for his family.

John took to it easier than his brothers. His early training – out of school more than in – prepared him for a life that would soon get much more difficult.

However, his natural childhood curiosity kept John's life from being just hard times and hunger.

He loved soccer. It was the favored childhood sport in Belgium and he excelled in it.

From his earliest memories, birds fascinated John. Whenever he had free time, away from school and his chores, he headed to the fields to find them. Whether it was their ability to fly away or simply to live in the moment, they appealed to the very core of his heart.

John's happiest moments came when he observed birds in their nests. His first discovery was a pair of long-tailed tits building a nest. The hundreds of feathers used to line their nests fascinated him. He saved his money to buy a pair of binoculars.

He spent hours at local nature reserves such as the De Liereman Bird Sanctuary.

As a budding birder, he drew the interest of adult enthusiasts. Several people took him under their wings and taught him about bird observation and identification, their habits and habitats, and banding and recording. A willing student, he lapped up their collective knowledge.

John Bax

John's red hair earned him years of childhood teasing. Coupled with his natural shyness, John felt most comfortable out in the fields exploring nature. "I sweated a lot every time I had to give a school report. I never wanted to draw attention to myself."

It would be years before John conquered his shyness. He found it almost impossible to speak to groups of people. "I took six aspirins if I had to speak. It helped some," he recalled.

Boys went to work early. Menial work was always available and John secured a job at the paper factory.

The first day on the job, John worked for what seemed like a long time and thought it must be time to go home. He looked at the clock and it was only 9:00. John decided that kind of work was not for him.

When large stacks of paper were trimmed, John's job was to cull the good cuts from the bad.

He raised crows at home. That first day, the crows followed him to work. When his shift ended, he went outside and the crows were gone – one more thing to convince John that this would not be a career choice.

Other happenings in 1925

Calvin Coolidge said, "The business of America is business."
"Dinah" and "Sweet Georgia Brown" were hit songs.
Louis Armstrong and Duke Ellington made their first recordings.
Lawrence Welk started a new band.
Roger Hornsby won the Triple Crown in baseball.
Nellie Ross, of Wyoming, became the first female governor in the US.
"Rin Tin Tin" and "The Phantom of the Opera" opened at movie theaters.
40,000 Ku Klux Klan members marched in Washington, DC.
Flagpole sitting became a national fad.
Earl Wise invented the potato chip.

From http://law2.umkc.edu/faculty/projects/ftrials/scopes/y1925.htm

Chapter 2: War Reaches Belgium

"The king just surrendered...there was no fighting." John Bax

In 1933, Adolph Hitler was named the Chancellor of Germany. A mere two months later, he became dictator and in 1934, he became Führer (meaning leader — a title Hitler granted to himself). In 1938, Hitler took over command of the Army and Germany took over Austria. In March of 1939, Hitler's Army invaded Czechoslovakia.

On September 1, 1939, when Germany invaded Poland, England and France declared war on Germany. Belgium announced its neutrality two days later. In November, the King of Belgium and the Queen of the Netherlands made a public appeal for peace. Belgian citizens continued their lives as they heard stories about the Nazi government and life in the countries the Germans conquered.

Some thought that Belgium's neutrality would keep them safe. Others felt that Hitler wouldn't stop until he controlled all of Europe.

John and his family spent most of their time trying to make ends meet. John went to school, poached with his dad at night, and spent his free time alone in the fields.

In April 1940, the Nazis invaded Denmark and Norway. Then, on May 10, 1940, they invaded France, Belgium, Luxembourg and the Netherlands.

Eighteen days later on May 28, King Leopold of Belgium surrendered against the advice of his government. He knew his troops were outnumbered and outgunned from the beginning. According to www.history.com, "Disregarding the odds, King Leopold III of Belgium had tried to rally his forces, evoking the Belgian victory during World War I. The Belgian forces fought on, courageously, but were continually overcome by the invaders."

The Germans refused his request for an armistice and demanded unconditional surrender. The King remained in Belgium as a prisoner of war.

Even though the government renounced his surrender, Winston Churchill supported his actions. Government officials went into exile and continued to support the Allied countries through an underground organization.

Thus began the Nazi occupation. Life immediately changed for all citizens.

John was fourteen years old.

King Leopold's surrender incurred the vehement condemnation of the majority of the Belgian people and brought accusations of treason. Leopold's decision to capitulate would plague him for the rest of his life.

At the time, the Belgian government-in-exile refused to acknowledge defeat and declared the King's surrender "illegal and unconstitutional". By the 30th May, the ministers had voted to divest Leopold III of all powers and of the right to rule.

http://noviomagus.tripod.com/leopold3.htm

Surviving Nazi Occupation

"Life was German soldiers, hunger and thousands of planes." John Bax

The children of World War II grew up to live with the scars of war – much like their parents and the soldiers who fought the battles.

Hunger was the immediate price children paid. Many lost parents and family members. All who lived under Nazi occupation lived in constant fear. They knew nothing of the terrible atrocities that came to light later.

John's memories were immediate and personal. He was always hungry.

With the war all around him, poaching and begging became crucial. John's father taught him more hunting skills. As a black market for food sprang up, it became a source of much-needed income.

He hunted small game and either took it home to his family or sold it. He set snares at night and worked in the factory during the day.

He crossed the border into Holland and smuggled in bread, butter, grain and potatoes.

To reach his destinations in Holland, John climbed over eighty-two barbed-wire fences. He was fast — running, climbing barriers, and finding places to hide. Once the police picked him up and took him to a detention center. It took his parents four days to raise the money to pay the fine for his release.

His dad sometimes went with him. Once when the Customs officials caught them, his dad fought. An official shot him and he acted like his injury was worse than it was to give John a signal to get the poached goods and hide them. The officials worried about his dad's injury and John understood his tactic.

His dad helped get money from farmers for the White Brigade; the underground that helped Allied soldiers escape. These underground groups occasionally became overzealous and used force to convince the farmers.

John's dad helped the White Brigade. John's grandfather was a hero working with the Underground in WWI. He died helping. His grave will never be exhumed, like most in Belgium, because he is a hero.

"My dad badly injured someone and served two years in jail after the war," John remembered. While his dad raised a vegetable garden in prison, at home the family's situation became ever more desperate.

"There was no time for fun. It was just surviving," John related. "One time the Germans came to our house. They told my brother to get in the truck. I went instead."

En route, airplanes sprayed the truck with bullets. John turned his head to the man in the next seat in time to see bullets rip into his head. Several others died including the crew's German chauffeur. John took charge and served as crew boss for the rest of the day.

The White Brigade

The beginning of the Nazi occupation saw thousands of Belgians deported to Germany as forced laborers and Jews shipped to Auschwitz. Two national resistance underground organizations arose: the White Brigade and the Secret Army. Throughout the war, these concerned citizens helped Allied soldiers escape from the Germans and furnished war information to the Allied forces. They played an important role in survival and Germany's defeat.

The Canadian army worked with the White Brigade in the opening of the port of Antwerp after the German army was ousted. John would later become a Canadian citizen.

"John was a survivor; he was strong minded even though he was shy with people," Alice Bax, John's wife, said.

John's sense of responsibility for his mother and brothers drove him to become more aggressive in his dangerous and illegal activities. He worked at any job he could find. Sometimes work took him to other European countries.

"I remember seeing Russians working in a field in France. If we had bread with us, we secretly threw it to them. There was a concentration camp in Antwerp. I didn't know what all went on there, but I knew that the guards didn't care about the prisoners," John recalled.

"Planes. Thousands of planes. German and Allied planes. We were afraid of bombs. They came every day. I remember the curfews — no lights. German soldiers in the streets."

"One of my fellow smugglers was a girl named Elizabeth. We got caught together one time. The Germans took us to a castle and we scrubbed floors for our punishment."

John and Elizabeth married shortly after the war ended. He was nineteen; she was sixteen. "I loved Elizabeth from the first moment I saw her. Her mother was against our relationship and didn't want Elizabeth to marry me."

John's memories of specific events remained strong. He recalled curfews and the dark — no lights were allowed at night. A German soldier shot at him once. He was caught stealing and taken to the castle again. When he was sixteen, a Jewish family asked him to help them escape to Sweden. They had come to Belgium from Holland. John agreed. They planned the route and headed out at night.

"The Germans caught us. The family tried to pay off the guards but it didn't work. The Germans told me to go home but they kept the others. I don't know what happened to them but I've often wondered. I don't think they survived."

> At John's memorial service, Esther Hughes, Alice's long-time friend, told the following story:
>
> "My daughter interviewed John for a school project about people in history. She asked him about his experiences in WWII. He told her about a time that he helped two men across the border out of Belgium.
>
> She asked, "How could you do that - put yourself in danger?"
>
> "How could I not?" John answered.

The world of John's youth required stealth and patience. Belgium had outlawed hunting because all the land was privately owned. John continued to hunt but made a silencer for his gun. He spent much of his time evading capture. When he wasn't hiding, he ran, sometimes for miles. He either developed, or naturally possessed, a heightened sense of his surroundings.

As the war raged on, John's chances of capture escalated. Returning to work one day, he saw Germans hauling off men to work in a munitions factory. He knew that many men were killed when the Allies bombed the factories.

John escaped to France to get away from the threat of working in a munitions factory. In France, he worked on an airfield for the Germans. Traveling throughout Occupied Europe opened his eyes. He witnessed and was part of several bombing attacks.

He watched the Germans load trains with workers. He knew that bombs hit many of those trains. In France when he was working in the forest, sixteen planes flew over and attacked the German trucks. Each plane dropped a couple of bombs. John ran into a bunker and prayed.

Once in France, he saw wrecked trains on top of each other. "I remember the V1 and V2 German bomber planes."

When the Allies liberated France and Belgium, John moved back to Belgium. Like most Europeans, he was desperate to gain control of his life and move past the war.

John possessed a natural business sense. Combined with an adventurous spirit, healthy energy and a growing self-confidence, it enabled him to grasp opportunities as they arose. If he wanted to do something, he made it happen. Early on, he developed those skills and sharpened them throughout his life.

"At the end of the war, I sold ice cream. One day I had some left and took it to the Allied soldiers. They bought it all. I went back with more the next day. I carried it on my bicycle. When I saw that I could make money that way, I started selling other stuff too."

****

No Longer Silent: World-Wide Memories of the Children of World War II is an anthology of the recollections of people who were children during the war. There's a great similarity no matter where they grew up.

> *During the entire period of occupation, I cannot remember a single day that I did not feel hunger. A Russian boy.*
>
> *I'd hang on the back of Dutch trucks. I'd hang on the German trucks. I stole everything... I ripped off everything I could, stole like a rat the last years. I had to... It wasn't easy either because the Germans would shoot you. They didn't care. They would absolutely open fire at you.*
>
> *I also stole collectively with packs of boys my own age. Cars that went around with food in them were especially good targets. We attacked with clubs and whatever... You see, it was survival – really sort of like an animal jungle. We just did what we had to do. The worst scene in the world is when there is no food and you are cold...*
>
> *Even my grandfather and I went out stealing... Lucien Hut, The Netherlands*

Food shortages in town and cities. Both in the country and in towns the Germans kidnap Polish young men and women to work in German factories and farms. Zofia C. Tarlowska Jancewicz, Poland

Tony Mercieca, photographer and John's good friend, grew up on Malta. War came to Europe when he was a toddler.

Although I was a little boy during WWII, I remember the airplanes and the bombs. I was born in Gzira, Malta, and lived there until our house was bombed. Dad moved us to a small town. There were bluffs nearby. Dad took the whole family out to help build a shelter. We actually chiseled out a cave. Dad gave me a small chisel and hammer and I remember banging away, doing my share. We spent lots of time in the shelter and always worked to make it bigger.

I remember planes falling down from the sky and bombs that hit close to our shelter. Sometimes they made holes in the hard rock. I helped carry water. We had a community faucet where we filled buckets and hauled the water to the cave. I had a wooden yoke over my shoulder with a bucket on each end. My buckets were little compared to my dad's. I think I always spilled most of my water. Toward the end of the war, food became scarce and everyone in our village was hungry.

The British and Americans made bombing raids from our country, first on Rommel's troops in Africa and later in Italy. - Tony

> Malta is an island country in the Mediterranean Sea off the toe of Italy. During WWII, the country was part of Britain's Commonwealth of Nations. It gained independence from Britain and became a republic in 1974. The island is comprised of 120 square miles and is home to more than 417,000 people. Maltese and English are the official languages.
>
> Malta has been strategically important throughout history and during WWII, it became home to British and American air operations.
>
> Today Malta is recognized as an internationally renowned tourist destination. It is home to some of the oldest freestanding structures in the world.

****

The loss of a childhood and an education angered John. Young people who took life for granted easily irritated him. Alice repeatedly told him that his childhood gave him strength, taught him determination and enabled him to pursue his dreams.

Although life was hard, John knew that the years of running through fields, climbing fences, working in factories, scrambling for food, and walking through the woods prepared him to walk for miles and carry heavy film equipment. The time he spent alone or hiding to evade capture taught him patience and the ability to wait and watch in stillness. The harsh financial conditions taught him to live frugally and save his money.

All of these would prove invaluable to John the cinematographer.

The War Ends, 1945-1955

"Food was still our #1 concern after the war..." John Bax

The war ended in 1945. John was nineteen. The years following the war brought good times and bad in his life.

When Allied soldiers occupied Belgium, they sold everything in sight. Like Belgian citizens, soldiers had faced long-term hunger. They confiscated anything they could find that might sell or buy food. Money and food remained scarce for several years.

Belgium required young men to serve one year in the Armed Services. John served his mandatory year and left with the rank of Corporal. He continued to work at the factory by day and poach rabbits by night. Though he had little education, his natural curiosity and wit spurred him to a lifetime of learning. He was the quintessential self-taught man.

He became a precision cutter at the paper factory. Life settled into a rhythm and all was well until the work ran out. John was laid off.

John and Elizabeth loved each other but trouble in their relationship started early.

They lost their first child and would later lose twin girls.

"Her mother caused our problems," John said. "She never wanted us to be together and she worked hard to tear us apart. She was extremely controlling and we let it eat away at our relationship. I wasn't a good husband."

John and Elizabeth had four boys: John Jr., Leo, Emiel, and Joseph. They remember their dad as strict and both parents as uncommunicative.

Chapter 3: The Good Years, 1955–1965

"I began to study the birds in earnest... I learned from experts." John Bax

In 1955, John started working at Philips, a lamp manufacturing company. Good pay brightened his life. He soon became an underboss in a new factory. Although sent to a new Holland factory to interview for management, he didn't get the job. He lacked the educational credentials.

During these years, John's interest in birds never waned. He joined the Oriole Society, the *Wielawaal.* (He was later named one of two honorable lifetime members.) He studied the birds and led outings.

He learned to identify birds. He helped research various species. He learned how to catch them with nets and band them. He wanted to know every aspect and characteristic of a bird's life cycle and living habits.

My best-known student was John Bax...who became a famous bird cinematographer.
- Willem Paulussen

He saw new birds. He remembered seeing a Black Woodpecker and a Noble Lapwing in Holland.

John met Willem Paulussen, a school principal, who collected bird eggs. John tagged along with him, learned how to locate the nests, and studied the nesting habits of different species. He soaked up Willem's expertise and gained invaluable experience in finding nests.

Willem built an impressive collection of bird eggs, which he later sold to a Belgian museum. His book, *The Breeding Birds of the Turnhout Campine*, shared his lifelong career of bird watching.

"I remember the day I found a tree falcon nest," John recalled. "I immediately found Willem and told him. He went back with me. I climbed the tree and brought the nest down to photograph it, then took it back up."

Willem was the president of the *Wielewaal.*

John's expertise grew.

John had no money to buy a camera. It would be years before he started filming.

****

Even with birding, life lacked the excitement of the war years. Poaching and smuggling had been necessary, but also a great adventure. John missed the adrenaline rushes that accompanied the threat of capture and escape.

John continued to poach even though the war was over. He brought rabbits home and put them in the basement. He sent John Jr. to market with them before he went to school.

"I remember the poaching." John Jr. said. "I was the one who had to take the rabbits and pheasants to market. Mom was into the smuggling with him during the war. Her mom made her go with him and work with the Underground to get food from Holland. She didn't approve of Dad's continued poaching after the war.

"Our grandmother didn't like Dad. She always wanted him out of our lives."

Their standard-of-living improved. John rode his motor scooter to work every day. John Jr. and Joe had bicycles. In 1964, John purchased his first car and the boys were ecstatic. "I remember it," Emiel said. "It was a 1963 Citroen and Dad was thirty-nine."

"I was always close to being late to work with the scooter," John remembered. "The car changed that."

John bought the family's first television in the late 1950s. Belgium had little programming at the time and most shows were produced in America. By the time they moved in 1965, *Bonanza* was their favorite show.

"Dad turned the television on and he turned it off. We never sat in his favorite chair. None of us wanted to make Dad mad. He was very strict." Leo remarked that the family didn't communicate well. "Mum had a lot of physical ailments and Dad didn't talk much. As children, we were left to our own entertainment. We played soccer and roller-skated. We loved to walk in the woods where we experienced nature and a sense of freedom."

****

John remembered that his dad would tell him that he would take him fishing in the morning. John would lay awake all night in anticipation – then his dad would change his mind. John never forgot his disappointment. He wanted to do better for his sons.

Every weekend John took one of the boys fishing, birding, or camping. "I liked it," said Emiel, "because we usually rode on his motorbike but there was always tension." The boys responded differently to these adventures.

Joe hated the bird-watching trips. He found them boring. "When the weather was bad, I refused to go unless Dad paid me. He did and then I had to go," Joe remembered.

As an adult, Joe became a birdwatcher and even appeared in one of John's films.

Leo only remembered fishing with his dad two or three times. Joe remembered one time and would have preferred the fishing trips to birding.

John loved being alone. "If he wasn't working, he was out birding or fishing," Joe said. "I felt like he always wanted things his way. He was never cruel and he never beat me. I guess the best way to describe it is that he wasn't interactive."

Emiel wanted to be part of his dad's life and learned to participate in his activities whenever he had the opportunity. He played soccer and he longed for John's interest and support. "I don't remember Dad ever coming to a game. I wasn't a good student and I wanted him to appreciate something I did well."

The Decision

"I wanted adventure...to study birds in other environments." John Bax

A continual restlessness haunted John's heart and mind. He had a good job and his family was growing. He made enough money to pay living expenses, and to start a savings account.

He spent all his spare time either with other members of the Oriole Society or out in the woods on his own.

John wanted something more. He started thinking about other countries – far away countries where he'd find new species of birds to study. He had the itch to explore and discover new opportunities.

"I needed to learn English." John traipsed out in a field to drill himself in English word pronunciation. He avoided practicing in front of his family and friends.

He settled on Australia because it sounded like a grand adventure. He investigated a program that provided free passage to Australia if you committed to living there for two years. He'd have to quit his job but he was confident he'd find something once he arrived.

He told the family. Another war erupted – this time in his own household. Elizabeth didn't want to move. She was an only child and didn't want to leave her mother.

The boys fought against it. They were growing up and Belgium was home. They didn't want to leave their friends, school, or life as they knew it.

When another family in town announced they planned to immigrate to Canada, John changed his mind. He'd take his family to Canada instead of Australia.

John wanted adventure and more opportunity for himself and his family. They wanted to stay put in their comfortable and pleasant hometown.

What to do? John wrestled with his decision — his wife and family on one side, his wanderlust on the other.

Life and work continued while John dreamt of the future.

A New Life in Canada

"I became Canadian...absorbed the language and culture, discovered its nature." John Bax

In 1965, John made the decision. He quit his job, sold everything, and moved his family to Canada. They made the journey with the other family who later returned to Belgium.

Even another family didn't abate the anger emanating from John's wife and sons throughout the long days on a boat crossing the Atlantic Ocean.

Elizabeth hated everything about the move. Her sons were upset, her household turned upside down — but her husband thought it was a great adventure.

John, Jr. at fifteen showed the most anger. He had finished school and signed up for the Air Force in Belgium. "Dad stopped it and made me move to Canada with them. I was furious."

"We all wanted to stay in Belgium, Mum included." Leo recalled the move. "Dad made us go. He talked about Canada, the land of cowboys and Indians, and promised us a pony. I remember my disappointment when I saw neither cowboys and Indians nor the pony." Leo's twelve-year-old mind had pictured Canada as *Bonanza* country.

Nine days on a boat must have seemed like months to the Bax family.

After the boat landed on Canadian soil, John took his family by train to London, a city of 136,000, which was home to a Philips Lamp factory. The Bax family started their new life in Canada the same year the maple leaf was adopted as the national flag symbol and the Canadian actor, Christopher Plummer, played Captain von Trapp in *The Sound of Music*.

"I had plans for my boys. I wanted to give them more opportunity. I knew they would have more career options in Canada than in Belgium. So I set a rule that all of us would speak only English at home. They hated it but they learned the language.

"I soon found out that the English I had learned was totally different than what I found here. I started practicing the 'new' English."

Applying for work at Philips was an obvious choice for John. He'd spent over ten years working for them in Turnhout. He liked the company and the work.

The boys enrolled in Canadian schools, became proficient in English, and slowly adapted to life in a new country. Years later they would recall the heat of those first summers. "Canada wasn't like *Bonanza* at all," Leo said. "As a seventh grader in a new country, I found lots of bullies. My brothers and I still wore the short pants like we did in Belgium. I got beaten up more times than I can remember."

Memories swarmed as Leo thought of his first days in Canada. "It was hot and humid. Not only did we not see cowboys, we couldn't speak English. The cars were huge. Nobody spoke to me on the boat ride from Belgium. It was a lonely time. I missed visiting my grandmother and everything about Belgium."

With the resilience of youth, Leo found school to be much easier in Canada than in Belgium where he attended half a day on Saturday and every weekday until 5:00 pm.

"It took me a year or two before I was comfortable communicating in English."

Joe said, "I turned eight on the boat when we moved to Canada. I don't have any bad feelings about leaving Belgium except I missed my grandmother.

"I didn't have much of a problem learning English. I think it took about a year before I was comfortable. I do remember a funny story though. We call it our 'hello story.' We all went to the park and spoke to everyone. We asked people how to say 'hello' in English. Finally someone told us and we started practicing it every time we met someone. We got beat up a few times before we learned that what we'd been told was 'hello' was actually an obscenity."

Life Changes

"I was mad at Dad for years." John Bax Jr.

Elizabeth didn't adjust to the move. She made several trips home and eventually, she and John went their separate ways.

"There was no affection in our family. I grew up knowing that I didn't want to get 'the look' from Dad," Leo said. "My parents separated while I was in college. It was tough on the family."

Though today Leo jokes about the "missing pony," at the time it created another reason to distrust his dad's promises. In the first months following the move to Canada, the pony issue loomed large in Leo's mind. It became symbolic of the lack of a relationship with his father.

Joe was the only one left at home when John and Elizabeth separated. "I was fifteen when he left. Since he was always after me to do better in school, I thought it would be a holiday without him. However, Mom just slapped me a lot more."

John Jr. remained angry for years. When he started working in Canada, he bought his own color television. He put it in his own room and would never let his dad watch it. "When Dad wanted to watch a bird show in color, I wouldn't let him."

On the other hand, as Emiel grew up, he liked visiting his dad. Both enjoyed running and it was something they could do together. "That was one thing we had in common. Dad introduced me to the outdoors. I loved to go hunting and fishing with him, too."

John loved his canoe. The boys named it the "bird van." Joe borrowed it to take a group of kids out on the lake. "Dad told me to tell the kids that if anything happened to stick with the canoe because canoes don't sink. They sank the canoe and it ended up at the bottom of the lake. Dad didn't say much but he brought down some oars to get it out. I hired some divers who brought the canoe up. Dad gave it to me. A year later, he wanted to buy it back."

Years passed before the boys talked to their dad about the move. Eventually they each established their own careers and became Canadian citizens. John Jr. is an electrician. Emiel, the second son spent his career as a factory worker. Leo, the third son, is an accountant — and Joe, the youngest, is a truck driver.

John had nine grandchildren and three great grandchildren.

City of London, Ontario

London, Ontario, was founded in 1836 at the Fork of the Thames River in Southwestern Ontario. Located 112 west of Niagara Falls, the city is situated approximately halfway between Toronto, Ontario, and Detroit, Michigan.

Chapter 4: New Opportunity

"I learned how to use my camera and how to film the birds." John Bax

As the days turned into months, John found plenty of time to explore the countryside and look for the birds. Over the next years he explored Canada in an ever-widening circle.

As a child, he saw the Disney movie *Fantasia*. He watched the grebes dancing on the water. John was awestruck. That film stuck with him his whole life. He loved Disney. In 1937, *Snow White* was released. John saw the movie over and over before the war. The more he watched movies, the more they fascinated him.

Fantasia led to a decision that would impact the rest of his life. Years later, when he moved to Canada he finally took money from his savings and bought a Super 8mm movie camera – a 12.5-power model.

"I read books and taught myself, starting with a Super 8 movie camera," John recalled.

John's journey began!

For the next four years, he spent every free moment outdoors with his camera.

He knew birds. There were different species to learn, but he had spent his life learning their ways. He studied their migration and their nesting habits.

He developed skill with the camera, an eye for lighting, setting and spatial relationships, and knowledge of the birds in Canada. Most importantly he utilized the patience and stillness he developed during the war. He discovered the advantages and limitations of Super 8mm technology.

At the factory, John talked about his exploits. He taught his fellow workers about birds and shared his films.

He filled roll after roll of film, keeping detailed notes of species found, places, times, and weather conditions. He saved everything.

****

He saved money from every paycheck to buy better equipment.

A friend introduced him to a man from the local television station who invited him to the station for an interview. He asked John to bring some of his film.

John agreed. The staff at the television station loved his work and encouraged him to continue filming. They recommended that he buy a 16mm camera. He knew it was time to spend some of his savings on a new camera.

"In 1969, I bought a 16mm camera. I didn't have the money to buy the lens to go with it." John bought a Bolex 16mm film camera – body only. He worked another year, saved his money and bought an $850 French lens – a 10mm and a 235mmx9. And so, John officially began his career as a nature cinematographer.

Produced in Switzerland, the Bolex cameras were particularly important for early television news, nature films, documentaries and the avant-garde, and are still favored by many animators today. Whilst some later models are electrically powered, the majority of those manufactured since the 1930s use a spring-wound clockwork.

The more John filmed, the more he loved the ability to use cinematography to capture the beauty of nature. He liked to experiment with the position of the camera, the angle of light, and the effect of the background.

He met and visited with other photographers. From them he learned that he had a knack for finding birds. As they taught him the tricks of photography, he taught them the habits of the birds. It became a life-long symbiotic relationship.

The television station expressed continued interest in his work. He knew the time was right to make a film — and he chose nesting birds as the topic.

John with a Bolex camera

One of his favorite memories from this film involved a waxwing that actually let him get close enough to feed him.

In 1971, he sold his film, *Nesting Birds*, to the Audubon Society. For the first time, John's work reached international television audiences.

John made another career decision at this point. The Audubon Society, when purchasing his film, offered to pay him for the work or to pay him royalties. John's independent nature left him only one choice. He wanted as much control of his life and filming as possible. He chose to sell the film on royalties. That allowed him to continue to make decisions of "when, where and what" to film.

He met Bob Bocking, a cinematographer and editor with the Audubon Wildlife Theatre series, produced by KEG Productions of Toronto, Ontario. Bob and John would work together on films throughout their careers.

Still working at Philips, John started immediately on a second film — *Birds in Ontario*. He sold this film to Wildlife Cinema in 1974.

He sold footage to Disney for a film on water birds. John knew this was his life's work and started planning for the day he could film full-time.

During these years, John found hummingbirds. There are none in Europe, so this discovery opened a whole new world. He fell in love with their beauty, spirit and characteristics. He began to look for different species and contemplated the idea that he could film birds all around the world.

John with trailer and camera

He bought an Airstream trailer and over the years, pulled it over much of North America for filming sessions. During the winters, he stored the trailer and lived in a motel. Knowing he had a home near the birds waiting for him helped him make it through the winter.

John worked full-time and filmed in his vacation and off-hours until his retirement in the late-1970s.

In Search of Hummingbirds

"I went south to find and study the hummingbirds. They captured my imagination." John Bax

John's search for filming opportunities took him first to the northern United States and later to the south. He pulled his trailer and stayed for weeks or months, wherever the birds led him.

"I wanted to learn more about migratory patterns and I wanted to follow the hummingbirds. I also wanted to find and film the Least Grebe," John explained.

In 1984, he set out from London, Ontario, to Big Bend National Park in south Texas. After spending a month, he traveled to Rio Hondo in the Rio Grande Valley where he set up his trailer for the winter. He stayed five months and fell in love with the area. After traveling south for several years, he moved to the Valley in 1991 where he became a full-time resident. He spent the last twenty-five years of his life filming in the southern US, Mexico, and Central and South America.

On one of his early trips to Arizona, he met Tony Mercieca. Their lifelong friendship began. In their travels together, John found the birds. He and Tony took turns — John filming and Tony taking photographs.

John's fascination with Arizona and southern Texas grew as he discovered the diverse species that reside in or migrate through those states.

He filmed hummingbirds in Madera Canyon in Arizona and throughout south Texas. His travels also led him to rare and never-before-filmed birds in Central and South America.

In 1992, he filmed hummingbirds in Brazil; in 1997, in Jamaica and Cuba.

One of his major goals was to film the Bee Hummingbird, the smallest species found only in Cuba. With a guide who found the hummingbird on a nest, John filmed the bird for a couple of days. He finally achieved one of his life's goals but at the time of his death, it had not been produced in a film.

His talent and dedication opened doors and his work resulted in major film productions.

Through him, Bob Bocking fell in love with hummingbirds. He visited John in Texas and worked with him on the KEG Production films, *Journey to Brazoria* and *The Man Who Loved Birds*.

Love Knocks Again

"Suave, charming and graceful with a captivating accent – those are the things I noticed in the first short dance." Alice Bax

John always enjoyed social activities. Through his love of ballroom dancing, he met Alice in 1984. They married in 1992.

"I lived in Harlingen (Texas)," Alice said. "In the spring of 1984, I went to a singles dance. One of the dances was an exchange dance where we had random partners. I partnered with John and in the short time we danced together, his accent and charm captivated me. He told me he had just come back from filming birds in Costa Rica. When we separated for the next partner, I knew I wanted to see him again."

The evening ended too soon. "We could do a lot more dancing," John told her.

"I know of a couple of places." Alice recalled dancing for several more hours that night. "I was ready to go with him anywhere he wanted to go by the time the evening was over."

John asked her out for the next weekend but cancelled when another woman friend came into town. Soon afterward, he returned to Canada for the summer. Alice continued attending dances and began dating another man.

Alice was an elder in her church, worked at Valley Baptist Hospital, and had a daughter, Jennifer, ready to enter junior high school. Her two sons were already living on their own.

In October at the singles dance, she saw John approach her table. "So how is Maria?" he asked.

"Who's Maria?"

"Isn't that your name?"

At this point, Alice almost refused to dance with him again. However, she did. At the end of the dance, he asked her out again. In an attempted brush off, she told him, "I don't have much time."

"I don't need much time," John's smile betrayed his confidence.

They continued going to dances throughout the winter. "I won't go out with anyone else if you'll be with me," John told her. She tried to remind herself that he was a smooth talker.

John made a film presentation at the RV park where he stayed in Rio Hondo. Its success led to years of visiting parks throughout the Rio Grande Valley. Alice accompanied him and helped sell his films.

He was meticulous in his planning. He approached it as a business. He accepted an offer to make monthly presentations and live at Fun n Sun RV Park in Harlingen.

Many of the park's residents became his friends. He led birding trips, found fishing buddies, photographers and couples who loved dancing as much as he and Alice. Fellow birder Glen Hindman called John "the Pied Piper of birders in the Valley."

John planned a trip to Brazil for December 1991. He would be there for three months. "How about you going with me?" he asked Alice.

Alice liked the idea but had only a couple of weeks to make arrangements with her church and work. Jennifer was away at college by then.

"Why don't you marry me?" John asked.

"I don't have time to think about that now." It was the first of several times that John proposed to Alice.

Finally, Alice agreed to the trip. While in Brazil, she wrote frequent letters home to her sons and daughter. One day John said, "I think I'll write to my sons." He sent letters to each of them. It turned a corner in his relationship with them.

John and Alice

The spring of 1992 brought a trip to El Cielo Biosphere Reserve in Tamaulipas, Mexico. Alice accompanied him. When they returned home, John proposed to Alice again. When she hesitated, he said, "I consider you my wife whether we're married or not."

Alice's reluctance to marry involved her children. She felt a need to make sure they were educated and independent before she worried about her own future.

Finally John asked, "Are you going to marry me or not?"

When she said yes, John asked, "Do I have to wear a ring?" Alice knew John didn't wear jewelry but said it would be nice. She never dreamed he'd actually do so. John surprised her when he told her he wanted to go pick out their rings.

Later John and Alice created and produced their own line of videos. John kept his camera gear ready to go bird watching when the weather was good or someone invited him.

With a blind and camera set up in his backyard, which was frequented by multiple species of birds as well as bobcats, coyotes and other animals, John gathered material for new productions.

John's extraordinary physical stamina resulted from a lifetime of running. From the poaching days of childhood to the discipline of adulthood, he ran. As an adult, he ran six miles a day, three times a week. At the age of seventy, he cut back to three miles a day; at seventy-two, he switched to walking. In his mid-eighties, he still walked thirty minutes a day.

Though he exercised and stayed fit, John's lifestyle didn't include healthy eating. He loved ice cream and ate it frequently. Next in line of his favorites was chocolate candy.

He had a family history of heart trouble. His two younger brothers died from aneurysms. Although he never had a heart attack, he did have an inoperable aneurysm, which led to his death on November 15, 2011.

Chapter 5: A Flood of Memories

"Dad didn't know how to interact with us." Joe Bax (youngest son)

John's four sons visited him just weeks before he passed away. The four of them shared memories of their dad. They agreed and disagreed as all siblings do. They remembered different things. Only Emiel remembered Leo's story of the missing pony.

Left to right: John Jr., Leo, Joe, and Emiel

As they talked, they pointed out that their father was not much different than a lot of other dads of that time. European men of the 1950s-1960s ruled their households.

Emotions flowed through the stories — laughter, humor, and hints of past anger and hurts. It was a day of coming together, reconnecting with the past, accepting the present and knowing this was most likely the last visit with their dad.

They all agreed that as young adults they had little to do with John. However, once John met Alice, he changed. He wanted to reconnect with them. They believe that Alice understood him and became an integral part of his life. She taught him to appreciate family.

They admired John's talent and his determination. What they deemed harsh as children, they respected as mature adults.

"We are all self-centered," Leo said. "I was angry with my dad for years but things have changed in the last eleven years. Most of it is due to Alice but some from my desire to communicate with him. I wasn't close to my mum either but I blamed my dad for our family problems."

John Jr. was the first of John's sons to visit him and Alice in Texas. He encouraged his brothers to visit. Joe and Leo and their wives visited. Later, John and Alice took many trips to Canada to reestablish relationships with his sons and their families.

Leo and his dad began sharing memories and finding common ground. "My dad was always very determined and goal-oriented. As a child I hated it but now I'm amazed by the things he accomplished. He taught himself everything he knows – about birds, filming, and the English language."

Joe discussed his relationship with his dad. "Things have been much better the last twenty years. We came down to Texas about fifteen years ago. Dad took us to all the refuges. I enjoyed it. I appreciate nature more now.

"One thing I've realized. Mom wasn't into birding at all. She would have inhibited Dad if he had stayed."

John Jr. admitted that he remained mad at his dad for years. "I really admire what he's done with his life. He has a real talent and he followed it. He taught himself everything he knows. That takes determination."

****

Although John had long ago forgotten the "pony promise," he had always been conscious of his failure to communicate with his sons. "I didn't want to be like my dad and it took me years to realize that I was. I had no real relationship with him and I failed to build one with my sons. I focused on work, learning English, adapting to a new culture, and studying birds."

Book Two: John's Filming Expeditions

"For decades, John Bax searched the world to bring us his beautiful images of nature and, in particular, his special passion – birds. A pioneer in nature cinematography, his work has been shared by millions. His odyssey has taken him all over the world – from the cold stark beauty of the frozen Arctic to the mist-shrouded mountains of the Tropics."

A Passion for Birds, Gorgas Science Foundation

Author's Note

"I guess I have a knack for finding birds and their nests." John Bax

Over coffee, hot tea and chocolate éclairs, John shared his early filming adventures.

"Tell her about getting lost," Alice encouraged. I smiled at her enthusiasm for stories she must have heard a thousand times. Throughout our conversations, she prodded his memory for the details of his early years.

"She's my assistant, you know."

"I bet she's a good one too," I smiled back at John.

Smiles played an important role in our interview sessions. Anytime John talked about his work, a smile lit his face. Alice laughed at each adventure and pulled out old photographs. Some days my face ached from so much smiling.

I smelled the heat and touched the cold as John related how he traipsed through the wilderness looking for birds. I marveled at the sights he'd captured on film.

"See that picture," John pointed toward the wall. "That's a Sword-billed Hummingbird that I filmed in Ecuador. Tony (Mercieca) took that. I think he's one of the top photographers in the world."

Our conversation bounced back and forth with little relationship to chronological detail. Memories colored John's dialogue as he led me helter-skelter through countries and bird species. When we stopped and looked at photos taken by his photographer friends, he talked about their skill and their art.

"I have some pictures on my computer. Seth (Patterson) taught me about the computer, you know." Pride colored his voice.

"I'd like another éclair," John told Alice. "How about you?"

I shook my head and concentrated on my notes.

"John likes chocolate." Alice put another éclair on his plate.

Chapter 6: John Spreads His Wings

"I remember the exquisite beauty of the loons...the thrill of filming thousands of Snow Geese." John Bax

In 1975, the University of Southwest Ontario planned an excursion to the Northwest Territory (the Arctic) to study Snow Geese and loons. Dr. Ankney, the assistant professor leading the expedition, invited John to accompany them.

"I couldn't miss the opportunity to film the birds. I took a three-month leave of absence from Philips." John said. "I paid my own way."

The group packed their heavy clothing in 45-gallon drums. They traveled by train from London, Ontario, to Churchill, Manitoba - a three-day trip.

In Churchill, they bought supplies and enough food to last for the three months. They waited for Eskimos to fly them in by helicopter to the McConnell Wildlife Sanctuary. It took seven trips to pack in all the people, food, and supplies.

"I remember the rough landing. We couldn't get in the first time and had to try again."

The cabins, sheds, beds, and furniture were flown in for their stay.

"I was assigned a top bunk in a shed. I learned that I suffer from claustrophobia and I couldn't breathe in the seven-inch space between me and the roof."

John's body reacted harshly. From that time on, he slept in the big cabin on a table.

He used an Arctic sleeping bag guaranteed to keep him warm in weather down to -40 degrees.

"The rivers had already broken up by the time we arrived."

> The McConnell River Migratory Bird Sanctuary is located in the Kivallig Region of Nunavut, Canada, in the land we know as the Arctic. The 32,800-hectar sanctuary (equivalent to 2.471 acres), is on Hudson Bay's west coast, 31 miles north of the Manitoba border. It is at the mouth of the McConnell River that flows to the Hudson Bay. The sanctuary is home to and an important breeding ground for the Lesser Snow Goose, Ross's Goose and the Canada Goose. It has been designated a Wetland of International Importance by the Ramsar Convention (an international treaty for the conservation of wetlands)

Snow covered much of the ground until June 21. When it melted, mosquitoes attacked. The repellent they used was a 95% DEET product called Muskol. It was strong enough to eat away at John's camera equipment. He had to take extreme care and tried to find that fine line between protection for himself and for his equipment.

In the beginning, the group maintained radio contact with the Eskimos. However, the equipment often didn't work and they couldn't depend on it. The Eskimos flew in several times to check on them.

While the students banded and studied the Snow Geese and loons, John filmed them — for three months, seven days a week.

John worked every day. He fished often and supplied the group with food. When it was too dark to film, he walked back to the camp and spent the evening with the students.

John worked closely with Larry Patterson, the photographer. When he set up a blind, Larry walked into the blind with him and then left. John stayed and the birds came, not realizing that someone remained in the blind. Sometimes fortune smiled on him and he was close enough to touch the birds and the eggs.

In the tundra, no trees grow. Lots of potholes proved dangerous and he had to constantly guard against tripping or falling. Under a foot of soil and growth, a bed of ice covered everything.

"There were twenty-one hours of daylight in June," John recalled. "The sun never goes beyond the horizon. It was great for exploring and filming.

"Every morning I walked until I found something I wanted to film. Then I set up my blind and went back to the cabin to get my camera. I explored the area up to eight miles from camp. I used just my camera (not his tripod) so I didn't have to haul so much weight. That meant I had to change positions every three minutes."

The students took nest samples. They collected eggs and brought them in to incubate. When the babies hatched, they studied their development, the ratio of their size to the egg size. They discovered that the bigger the eggs, the faster the growth.

Birds born in captivity imprint with humans. To successfully release the birds back into the wild, the students took them out to the tundra to feed several times before

> Imprinting is a term that describes how many animals decide 'who they are'. It is a critical behavioral process in a growing animal and occurs during a period in which the young establish the concept of "parent" and "self". Taking place early in life, it is an irreversible process.
>
> http://audubonportland.org/sanctuaries/wcc/stories/imprinting

turning them loose.

He enjoyed sharing the students' experiences and stories. He learned about their project and shared his filming with them.

"We joked about fighting the mosquitoes. We laughed about the cold, the food, and sleeping conditions. I liked them."

Near the camp, a creek flowed into the river. It proved to be a good fishing spot for John.

A couple of times when the Eskimos came in, they helped with the fishing. They also shot caribou and shared the meat.

"The mosquitoes didn't bother the Eskimos," John remembered. "We noticed that right away. But they bothered us. Mosquitoes and black flies. Sometimes, if there wasn't much wind, the flies would swarm us. If you swiped across your arm, you'd kill about 25 flies and mosquitoes."

John saved all of his raw film. The three months of filming produced three films of over 200,000 Snow Geese and loons.

He loved the experience, the scenes he captured —and the friends he made.

John showed his work to KEG Productions in Toronto. They planned to produce a one-hour special, but a reverse in finances caused them to back out of the project.

Untamed World, a Toronto-based organization that produced specials for German television, bought his film and turned it into two specials on the Arctic. They also bought footage from him for a special on Southwest Ontario.

Throughout his career, John would sell his work to worldwide shows including National Geographic, Audubon Wildlife Theatre, Untamed World, Lorne Green's New Wilderness, Profiles of Nature, Disney, PBS, and Discovery Channel. His work has also been shown on educational stations in England, Europe, Australia, and Japan.

The Arctic, 1975

"I was always interested in filming the loons." John Bax

John's meticulous note taking covered everything from expenses to bird identification. His dedication and perseverance stand out. Whether it is hypothermia, rashes, car trouble, or native cultures, he paints a picture of the day-to-day life of a nature cinematographer.

His world was one of solitude, extreme temperatures, aching muscles, heavy loads, and months at primitive and remote camping sites, working from daylight to dark, mosquitoes, and poisonous weeds. He met, filmed, and made friends of people he met on his travels.

One ledger is filled with notes from his trips from 1975–1983 and his life list as of 1988.

It's difficult to choose random passages from John's journal. Viewed completely, they tell the story of one man's exciting career. Almost every entry finds John searching for, or filming, birds. Join him on his adventures.

John's notes use the European-style date (day, month, and year). Below are excerpts from filming expeditions in the Arctic.

Daily Reports

Trip to the McConnell River NWT

The Party:

Dave Ankney	Assistant Professor
Janet Ankney	His wife
Theresa Ankney	Daughter (6 yrs)
Dave Kiell	Student
Larry Patterson	Photographer
Randy Seguin	Student
Jim Hawkings	Student
John Bax	Film maker
Jack (dog) from the Ankney's	

5-5-75 We leave London on the 7:50pm train to Toronto. In Toronto we took the Trans Continental to Winnipeg

(Manitoba) where we arrived 7-5-75

8-5-75 In Winnipeg we took the train to Churchill at 6:00pm

9-5-75 Still nice weather sunny and mild. In the Pass fishermen were catching lots of Pike, also a few pickerel were taken from the Saskatchewan River

Between the Pass and Thompson I was allowed to take pictures from the engine.

The Boreal Forest as they call it

contents: Black Poplar – White Poplar – Birch - Black Spruce and Jack Pine

Film Reports

(same time period)

Pictures of the University of Western Ontario – meeting Asst Professor Dr. D. Ankney.

Taken with 12-120 mm lens.

Try out standard camera at Long Point with 3 different lenses.

Pictures of meeting Dr. Ankney

6-5-75 Pictures of train trip Toronto-Winnipeg with 10mm lens and 12-120mm lens

Pictures taken in Winnipeg 12-120 mm

7-5-75 Building – park – the crew on this nice sunny day

8-5-75 Filmed the trains coming in and going out – leaving Winnipeg – trip from Winnipeg to the Pass with 12-120mm

9-5-75 Trip from the Pass to Thompson with 12-120mm.

Filmed fishing in the Pass – fishermen were catching lots of Pike and a few pickerel – filmed from engine – filmed dining room in train

****

The group spent a couple of days in Eskimo Point before heading to their campsite. While they waited, John filmed the people and learned about them. In his notes, he described the life of the Eskimos.

****

11-5-75 Sunday, we couldn't get out. The Eskimos spend most of the day in Church (Roman Catholic and Anglican). They all have ski doos and sledges – 3-wheel vehicles (Honda) and some still have the dogs. There were lots of caribou during the winter, they say, and meat was no problem.

They also shoot lots of wolves. They get them by running them down by ski-doo. Some of the Eskimos used 10 ski doos in one year because it takes about 1 ½ hours to get the wolf and one hunter killed about 300 wolves. One ski doo cost around $1200-$2100 but one wolf pelt sells for $75. The premium for the wolf kill was taken off this year.

****

When they finally arrive at their camp, John's notes continue day-by-day. Throughout the trip, he made both daily reports and film notes.

****

25-5-75 Sunny day, lots of Snow Geese are coming in, also Snow Bunting, Short-eared Owl (2), Old Squaws (now Long-tailed Duck) (2) Scaups (2) Pintails, Horned Larks, Lapland Longspur, Whistling Swans (now Tundra Swan), Ruddy Turnstone, Semi-palmated Sandpiper. 4200 Snow Geese were counted in 2 hours.

3-6-75 Cloudy. Found Ross Goose with 3 eggs and Canada Goose with 3 eggs. Found Snow Geese (blue phase)…

7-6-75 Sandhill Crane	2 eggs
Dunlin (3)	1-2-4 eggs
Canada Geese	4-5 eggs

8-6-75 Filmed Dunlin on nest. Set up blind by Sandhill Cranes. Birds came to nest within 45 minutes.

Jaegers robbed snow geese nest. Snow Geese pair tried to fight them away without success. The Jaegers eat 2 of the 3 eggs in the nest.

Sandhill Cranes were disturbing two Snow Geese nest but did not pick in the eggs, just picked up the feathers and tried to fight the Snow Geese out of their territory.

17-6-75 Crew going out to mark geese nests. Dave and Randy going away for 2-3 days to collect ground squirrels.

> 21-6-75 Mosquitoes are out
>
> 22-6-75 Willow Ptarmigan with two cameras and 10mm lens only 5" from nest. Snow Geese with three young. Snow and blue phase of Snow Geese eggs hatching in the incubator in camp.
>
> 23-6-75 The crew collecting eggs for incubator.
>
> Sandhill Crane on nest. One young out, other hatching. Snow Geese on nest (close up to 5'). One caribou.
>
> 24-6-75 Filmed Arctic Loon 8 hours in blind, after 7 hours other Loon showed up and the Loon leaves the nest. I believe other Loon started incubating.
>
> 26-6-75 Red Phalarope – 3 eggs. King Eider – 5 eggs. Sandhill Crane – 1 egg. Canada Geese 4 with 2 eggs each.
>
> 5-7-75 Sunny and warm. Caribou shot by Eskimos and taken by Honda into camp. Ate caribou for supper. Eskimos leaving after supper…
>
> 7-7-75 Winds up to 50 MPH, some sun, cold. 12 caribou (one little one). One with big antlers, looks kind of black.
>
> 17-7-75 Filmed the King Eider on the North Branch of the Mac Connell River. Saw caribou, caught 10 graylings in evening.

All too soon John's leave of absence came to an end. He needed to go home. He had shot 12,000 feet of film. Larry had taken more than 3,000 slides.

The group needed a few more days, so John tried to find some Eskimos to take him back to Eskimo Point. However, it was whale-hunting season and the Eskimos were working. When that failed, he decided to walk out. Larry offered to go with him.

> 27-7-75 Walked out with Larry Patterson from camp to Eskimo Point. We walked close to 40 miles because we did not follow the coast line and walked 10 miles too much…We saw Whistling Swans (now Tundra Swans) with 3 young also lots of Whimbrel and common Eider Ducks…We walked out of camp 4:00am and arrived in Eskimo Point at 7:00pm.

> 28-7-75 Normal flight was cancelled because of fog but at 8:00am I could fly to Churchill with a charter. I saw about 20 Beluga Whales close to Churchill on the flight over Hudson Bay.

From Churchill, John caught a flight to Winnipeg with a stopover in Thompson. In Winnipeg, he had to flag down the plane to catch it to Toronto. The last leg took him home to London.

****

Although much younger, Larry found it difficult to keep up with John. As many others would note over the years, Larry was amazed at John's personal drive and persistence. He returned to the rest of the group. Later he sent John a photograph of the loons they had observed together. It was the first of many photographs to decorate John's walls.

Canada, 1976

"I fell in love with hummingbirds." John Bax

In 1976, John filmed extensively in Canada around Middlesex, Norfolk, and Elgin Counties as well as Long Point, Fingal, and Georgian Bay.

In the northern locations, John loved to catch and cook fish.

It was during this time that he developed his life-long fascination with hummingbirds. This love would be the catalyst for many of John's sojourns over the years.

> 17-6-76 Short-eared Owls in Fingal Resort. I saw four owls that evening flying around when it was getting dark, at least two young, but I think there were three young judging by the darker colour of the young. One of the adults cried when I approached one of the young. The adult drove the male Marsh Hawk away when it came too close to one of the young.
>
> The Short-eared Owl started nesting around the end of April. Also nesting in the Fingal Resort are Sparrow Hawk (now called Kestral), Red-tailed Hawk, Meadowlark, Bobolink, Yellow-shafted Flicker. Three Turkey Vultures flying around.

On 12-7-77 he wrote:

Georgian Bay: The Ruby-Throated Hummingbird from 11-7 is building a new nest about 60 feet from 1st nest with the two young in. As I am filming the nest with the two young, I have a view of both nests.

The female works for about ½ hour on the new nest (feet in between) and flies from new nest to the nest with the two young in to feed both young. Probably the hummingbirds have 2 broods per year.

New nest is also in oak tree on horizontal branch about 25 feet high.

13-7-77 Ruby-Throated Hummingbird. Found a 3rd nest in birch tree about 20 feet high.

Manitoba, 1978/1979

"I went to film the grebes... I went back for years." John Bax

In 1978, John took another leave of absence from Philips and journeyed to Manitoba to film as many species of grebes as he could find. This work took several trips over the next couple of years.

As John traveled across Canada, he estimated that he covered a couple thousand miles in his canoe. In most of the early years, John traveled alone. As his work became known, he met photographers who came to work with him.

Excerpt from John's notes:

6-6-78 Ericson Area. Two couples of Red-necked Grebes checked for a nest on two different lakes but I believe it is too early.

Horned Grebes on many sloughs.
Pied-billed Grebe – 8 eggs.
American Coot – 5-6-9-10 eggs
Red-winged Blackbird – 3 eggs plus Cowbird egg

13-6-78 Waterhen - Manitoba. 12-120 mm zoom lens fell into the water – I tried to film the dance of the Western Grebe but I did not see or hear them.

14-6-78 trip to Winnipeg to have lens fixed (400 miles)

16-6-78 Waterhen. Western Grebes are swimming around with young on their back.

Waterhen, Manitoba is in the Central Flyway and is a first stop for migrating birds and waterfowl.

Black Crowned Night Heron: I was 4.5 hours in blind on nest with 3 young about 8 days old – parent did not show up – young were very comfortable (feed young after dark)

17-6-78 Waterhen. Western Grebe – filmed the dance of the grebes in open area into the marsh while other birds are incubating and swimming around with young on their backs.

18-6-78 Some pairs are still dancing on the water and act as they will start nesting – filmed this, also bird on nest.

Bolex tripod – leg broke off. I travelled to Winnepagosis to have it repaired.

20-6-78 Waterhen. Horned Grebes came back to the nest with 3 eggs 10 minutes after the blind was set up and the canoe was out of sight.

Canadian map courtesy of Dreamstime.

21-6-78 Waterhen. Red-necked Grebe – extreme care has to be taken when standing in blind, moving is not advised as I believe the adults check around my blind before going on the nest.

1-7-78 Lawrence Lake. Eared Grebes. Saw the nesting place of the big colony – about 70 pair. They all leave the nesting area very quickly when I come close. Blind was set up the day before and the birds came back to the nest in less than 20 minutes.

Saw five Avocets. They acted as if they had a nest around (see 3-7-78)

2-7-78 Horned Grebes. Filmed the birds on and around their nest. I put up the blind, pushed the canoe 20' away and stayed in the blind. Parents came back fast and changed every hour on incubating. When this happened they brought more nest material to build up their nest.

Saw the beaver again, resting on bed of reeds.

****

13-6-79. Sunny, warm 15-26 ° C.

Manitoba

Filmed Eared Grebe colony. The birds were very active with nest building, mating and egg laying.

I think about 50 pair started already in one area about 100 x 100 meters. Most were still nest building. About 20 nests: contents one egg; some with 2 eggs; and one nest had 3 eggs.

The birds made a soft sound like woe-oli-woe-oli. Also this species shook their wings on the nest and then laid down so mating could take place, usually after some more nest building was done by both birds.

Some Black Terns are nesting in the colony only one foot away from Grebe nests. When the Grebes came too close to the Tern nests, they were chased away...

****

John noted behavior and identification methods in his journals and films.

"Rails make a dome for nesting – look for the dome to identify – they don't fly on nest – they run," John explained in one of his films.

As John traveled in search of birds, he met photographers who accompanied him on his nature treks.

"I met Tony Mercieca during these trips," John related. "He wanted to photograph the grebes. On most of the trips I took over the next several years, Tony met me there.

"We spent a lot of time paddling in canoes. Tony used to tell people, 'John sits in the back and gives orders.' I still laugh when I think about those trips."

Over the years, John and Tony worked together many times including Jamaica, Canada and Texas.

Chapter 7: The 1980s

Costa Rica and Central America, 1981/1982

Car trouble and a mugging mar nature's beauty

5-10-81 Left London by car and trailer

6-10-81 Travelled all day and most of the night…gas prices in the US vary from $1.16 to $1.35 US per gallon.

7/1-/81 Arrived in Southern Texas…travelled about 1900 miles now.

9-10-81 Visited Santa Ana Wildlife Refuge…saw Lichtenstein (now Altamira) Oriole, Plain Chachalaca, Least Grebe, Ringed Kingfisher, Black Hawk, Green Jay…all new birds.

10-10-81 Crossed Mexican border…I noticed a lot of Black Vultures along the road and also Scissor-tailed Flycatchers and Loggerhead Shrikes.

11-10-81 Arrived in Queretera…drove through the mountains (2 summits) 5500 and 5700 ft. Hand-controlled trailer brake in car stopped working… Left Ciudad Victoria and pulled into Hotel Azteca at 5:30pm. I got stuck in the grass. On the road I saw dead dogs, cattle and a burro – lots of Black Vultures around also hawks and kestrels. Along the road I noticed families - children, women and men with hawks and falcons on their arms or in a cardboard box.

17-10-81 Crossed the border into Guatemala. First stop is the Mexican officials where I handed back all the papers I received when I got into Mexico.

20-10-81 Do a lot of walking – it seems I have a problem with the brakes of the trailer…Lots of kids around the trailer; they all want to see the inside.

22-10-81 Went bird watching…saw new birds. Amazon Green Kingfisher, Derby Flycatcher, Spot-breasted Oriole, Black Seedeater…unidentified hummingbird.

25-10-81 Walked up part of the mountain. Town here is dirty…

horses, cows, dogs and pigs all run in t he streets. Lots of Turkey Vultures around. New bird: Smooth-billed Ani (common).

26-10-81 New species: Great-tailed Grackle, Sumichrast's Blackbird, Broad-billed Hummingbird and White-winged Dove.

27-10-81 Mechanic tried to fix the electrical brakes but he could not do it… I decided to return to the US to have the brakes repaired.

Car trouble and bridge out to Honduras. Went back to Arizona to get brakes repaired.

28-10-81 Crossed the border of Guatemala. Not too much trouble with papers, inspection, etc… I parked for the night at a gas station close to Mazatenango. Two heavy explosions and much shooting woke me up. I left, closed the trailer and ran in the brush and a cornfield where I stayed for several hours… Sometimes shooting was nearby. A little before 3:00am, I went back to the trailer. Things were quiet after that... In the morning people stopped at the gas station and talked about it. They advised me to go straight ahead to the Mexican border and not to stop unless for an official.

29-10-81 Crossed the border into Mexico. Not too much trouble on the Guatemala side but one official on the Mexican border refused me a pen to fill out a visa permit. He wanted to send me back over the river to get one from an embassy in Guatemala but a higher official told him to give me a form…and a pen. Saw a new bird…White-throated Magpie-Jay.

3-11-81 Many things wrong with the car so I stayed in Texas for three days.

7-11-81 Travelled into New Mexico

8-11-81 Arrived in Arizona where I parked in a camping place close to Ramsey Canyon. Most of the hummingbirds had gone south but I saw three species: Anna's Hummingbird, Rivoli's (commonly called Magnificent) Hummingbird and Blue-throated Hummingbird.

11-11-81 New birds seen at Madera Canyon: Bridled Titmouse, Acorn Woodpecker, Mexican Junco, Oregon Junco.

13-11-81 New bird: Lesser Goldfinch. Took one picture of Blue-throated Hummingbird.

14-11-81 Sierra Vista, Arizona. Five new species for life list: Ash-throated Flycatcher, Bewick's Wren, Lark Sparrow, House Finch and Black-throated Sparrow. Also lots of jackrabbits and cottontails, Road Runner, Green Kingfisher, Loggerhead Shrike and Black Phoebe.

15-11-81 New bird: Ladder-backed Woodpecker. Another new bird in afternoon: Brown Towhee (now Canyon Towhee), Pacific Race.

18-11-81 One new bird: Common Bushtit. New animal: the Coatimundi.

3-12-81 Flew to Costa Rica. Arrived in Alajuela.

4-12-81 2 new birds: Delattre's Warbler and Inca Dove…also some hummingbirds (hung up 2 feeders).

5 -12-81 2 new birds: Blue Tanager and Cayenne Squirrel-Cuckoo.

6-12-81 Two new birds: Olive Grasquit and Hoffman's Woodpecker

7-12-81 New bird: Allied Emerald

19-12-81 I have been attacked by two young men, approximately 15 and 20 years old, on the property of the farm. They stood by one of my hummingbird feeders. We talked for a little while and then one asked for a cigarette… and finally for money. When I wanted to leave, they wouldn't let me and a fight started. I fell in the river with one … The only thing I lost in the fight were my glasses, which they took. I hurt one of my ribs.

20-12-81 I had to sleep in an armchair as I couldn't lie down in bed. It hurts my side.

22-12-81 Went for x-rays and learned that one rib was broken. A bone specialist examined me and put on an elastic girdle (to be on for five weeks)…He also told me that my blood pressure was high and that one valve of my heart did not close completely. (Two weeks later a heart specialist told me that nothing was wrong; that my heart was better than that of a person fifteen years younger).

John stayed in Costa Rica until March. He saw other new species including the Rufous-tailed Hummingbird and the Fork-tailed Hummingbird. Because his luggage was overweight and the cost of flying was high, he took a train to Limon, then a bus and boat to Tortugero where he saw three species of monkeys — howler, spider and white-faced.

He visited the Poás Volcano in Central Costa Rica. It is an active volcano. The crater's lake is one of the most acidic in the world.

14-1-82 Poas Volcano. Rivoli's Hummingbird or Magnificent HB. Filmed this bird. Simon's Hummingbird. Filmed this bird on the same flowers as the Rivoli's.

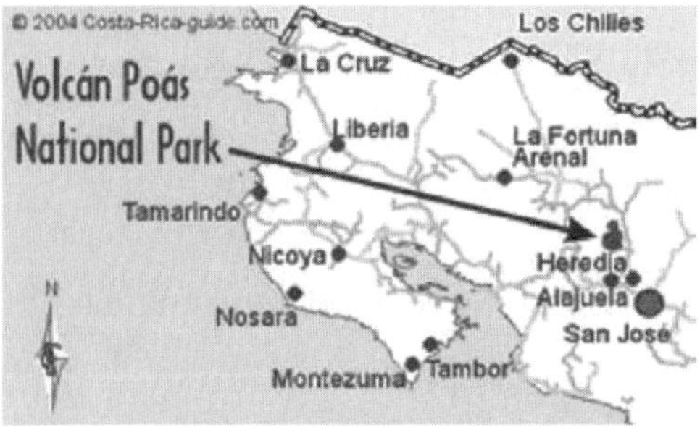

2-2-82 Went to Monteverde (a reserve where they study the hummingbirds. New birds: Minor Frigate (Great Frigatebird or Fregata minor), Blue-throated Toucanet, Lesser Violet Ear, Guatemalan Quetzal, Jalapa Trogon, Azure-hooded Jay. I met Dr. Peter Feinsinger who told me they had 22 species of hummingbirds.

9-2-82 New bird: Ferruginous Owl.

15-2-82 Cerro De La Muerte – Costa Rica. Filmed the Magnificent (Rivoli's) Hummingbird (64FPS) on another type of flower. The female came only two times in 3.5 hours. Also filmed some of the scenery… I will travel back to the (finca) farm tomorrow.

18-2-82 Stayed inside all day. My lips are bothering me… I have mailed films to Canada 4 x 100 ft. and 2 x 400 ft.

1-3-82 In the garden, the Allied Emerald sits on his usual place but beside it sits another Hummer, which feeds from the feeder. It is, I think, a Rufous-tailed Hummingbird.

6-3-82 Today, in the morning and for the first time, I have a Fork-tailed Hummer on the feeder.

19-3-82 Tortuguero – Visited park for two days. Saw three species of monkeys: Howler, Spider, White-faced. Also Peccaries (javelinas). One of them was making noise at me while the rest of the bunch ran away. Saw Rufous Hummingbird with nest and two young. New birds:

Ringed Kingfisher
Brazilian Great Black Hawk
Ruddy Ground Dove
Collared Aracari
Keel-billed Toucan
Massena Trogon (aka Slaty-tailed Trogon)
Lineated Woodpecker
Cande's Manakin
Giraud's Flycatcher
Gray-breasted Martin
Purple-throated Fruitcrow
Plush Tanager
Thick-billed Seed-Finch
Richmond Sparrow

The Massena Trogon male and female were nest building

21-3-82 Boat trip back. Saw an iguana – big and small…howler monkeys…alligators…stayed in Limon at the American Bar.

22-3-82 In front of the American was a park with sloths. I saw three and one of them was carrying a young. Left Limon and was back at the farm at 3pm.

26-3-82 Filmed the Rufous-tailed Hummingbird with 10mm and 12-120mm lens on feeder on 50 FPS with the lenses closed about three stops for special evening effects. Found nest of Cassin Dove. Bird is incubating.

3-4-82 Las Cruses, Costa Rica. The hummingbirds are all feeding on some kind of banana flowers of which they have 10 different kinds in the garden. Lots of birds are nesting. I have seen the Gray Robin on the nest and the Plush Tanager and White-tailed Tody Flycatcher were building. Also found hole in bank with three young.

19-4-82 Filmed oxcart on and around the farm; also filmed a house with many cans outside on the walls with flower (typical for Costa Rica).

One of the sons who was living about 20-25 minutes from his parents' farm where they had the oxcart, walked with me. One of the sons went in the mountain meadows to get the 2 oxen and they prepared the cart, after they ran it down the hill and back so I could take the pictures of this typical transport for Costa Rica. Also took some scenery in the mountains and a volcano in the distance located in Panama.

20-4-82 Filmed the Blue-throated Toucanet with 235mm lens. On nest hole.

27-5-82 Four nests of hummingbirds of which three were located in coffee plants in an area of 100x100 meters. Other nest was in a tree. The hummingbird visited and got on the nest twice. Nest #7 in coffee plants was empty and had 2 eggs earlier. Nest #8 (White-throated Mountaingem) had two eggs, the female was incubating. Nest #9 (Rufous-tailed Hummingbird) had two eggs, also this female was incubating. All nests were located less than 1.5m high.

John continued tracking these nests and noted empty or abandoned nests. By June 6, the nests were all empty. John did record the beginning of three new nests in coffee plants. Throughout his journals, he captured the nesting season with its triumphs and tragedies — from the hatching of hungry young chicks to broken or eaten eggs and dead chicks.

He recorded the lenses used and the raw film footage sent home to Canada.

3-9-82 By car to Toronto to see the film, had camera checked and lubricated, bought 16mm film (40' x 100') and went to embassy to pick up Visa for Ecuador.

Driving to Costa Rica and back caused plenty of damage to his car. He experienced most of the dangers that friends had warned him about, including ruined shocks and burned-up brakes. The mugging by the two young men left him with bruises and a broken rib.

John went back to Arizona in September where he stayed until his trip to Ecuador in November of 1982.

Two Creative Energies

"John and I shared great adventures and captured some amazing birds on film and in photos." Tony Mercieca

After John met Tony Mercieca, they enjoyed working together. An accomplished photographer, Tony loved to photograph the birds that John found and they worked together for the next twenty-five years.

"John has a sixth sense for finding nesting birds, more so than anybody I've ever seen," Tony said.

Tony Mercieca

In Arizona's Madera Canyon, Tony photographed several species of hummingbirds while John shot rolls of footage. In Jamaica, they found the Streamer-tail Hummingbird and Jamaican Mango. Tony had planned to travel to Cuba with John and Alice but the airlines crushed the special flash built to photograph hummingbirds and he had to return home.

"He never gave up," Tony laughed. "He found us some spectacular times." Tony related the story of his photo of a beautiful Great Gray Owl and her baby. "We were in Saskatchewan. John found a nesting pair of Great Gray Owls. They were on a nest about forty-feet up in a tree. The two babies jumped off the nest before they were fully winged. They landed on the ground. One died, from the fall I guess, and we never saw it. We found the other. The mother apparently found the dead baby, ate part of it and fed the rest to the remaining baby. John watched and filmed the whole process. In the morning I took pictures of the mother and her young. It's still one of my favorite photos.

"One year my wife Peg flew up to Saskatchewan to spend the summer with John, Alice, and me. John and I took the canoe out looking for kingfisher nests. We found one on the side of a bluff on the river. We wanted to film the young in the nest. However, the babies were far back in the nest hole. We went back another day. Someone or something had fallen through the ground and the nest hole had an opening in the top. John worried that the birds wouldn't survive the cold.

"Another time, it was bitterly cold. We found some Ruffed Grouse that were barely alive. Alice picked one up and cuddled it inside her blouse to warm it. We believe the babies survived."

Tony shared stories that are funny now but weren't at the time. One time John fell into a cold lake with his waders on. The waders filled with water and were so heavy that John had a hard time getting back in the canoe. Another time in Texas someone stole Tony's blind. Thefts are unusual and Tony missed an opportunity to take more pictures of nesting kingfishers in an old woodpecker hole. Since kingfishers usually build a cup-like nest, this unusual nesting site created a good photo shoot.

On one trip in Saskatchewan, Tony and John came across remains of a baby and a cow moose that had been killed. They assumed Indians did it because only parts of the carcasses were left.

In Manitoba, they were filming Common Loons from their canoe. Tony stepped onto a little island to take a picture and the island started sinking. Tony had his wallet in his pocket. By the time he made it back in the canoe, he was soaked up to his neck.

"One year when we filmed loons, I made a platform," Tony said.

John replied, "This won't work."

"Are you going to help or complain?" Tony asked.

Later John was the first to say, "This is great."

"Another time in Manitoba, we were pushing upstream in a canoe looking for Western Grebes. As John got older, he used a small electric motor on the canoe in case we needed it. We kept paddling against the current and still losing ground. John sat in the back of the canoe telling me to paddle...paddle. It became hard work."

When Tony looked at the motor, he discovered it was hooked up backwards. John said, "I'll turn it over."

"Just put it in reverse," Tony told him.

"No, I'll turn it over." He did and they went back to documenting the grebes.

Together they met noted experts in the field of ornithology.

"Through John, I met Dr. George Peck. He was a Research Associate in Ornithology at the Museum of Natural History in Toronto. He has written several books on birds and identified 300 nesting species. When John lived in Canada, he found and observed birds for him. He recorded the nests (especially on warblers), took notes on 3x5 cards, and turned them in to George for use in his books and for museum records. George came to the Valley a couple of times and the three of us took pictures together. I stay in touch with him.

"In Ecuador I met Dr. Fernando Ortiz, a famous ornithologist, who John had worked with earlier. He wrote a well-received paper about the serration on the bills of hummingbirds."

When John told Dr. Ortiz that he was going out to find the hummingbird nests, Ortiz replied, "I don't think you're going to do that. I've been trying for years."

John found several nests and took Dr. Ortiz to see them.

In Canada, the mosquitoes were bad and they constantly had to fight them off.

John loved to fish and considered it great fun. Tony remembers once when he caught a big pike.

Tony travels to South Padre Island every spring to film the migrating birds. "It was always a highlight to spend some time with John."

In October of 2011, when Tony received the news that John was ill, he drove from California to spend some quiet days with him. They reminisced about birds, photographs, and their many shared adventures.

Ecuador, 1982/1983

"I loved the sword-billed hummingbird." John Bax

John spent six months in Ecuador. In the first few days, he met with Dr. Fernando Ortiz, a hummingbird specialist from the Universidad Catholica in Quito.

Following Dr. Ortiz's advice, John found and filmed nesting Black-tailed Train Bearers and Sparkling Violet Ears, both hummingbirds. He marveled at the Sparkling Violet Ear nests made of lichen and spider webbing. He found hummingbird nests built by various species, checked them for eggs, and followed their progress day-after-day.

John recorded cultural activities everywhere he encountered something that pleased or inspired him.

The mountain villages spoke to him of serenity not found in the modern world. He loved the dignity and pride of the people, the descendants of the ancient Incas. The shy Inca children soon responded to John and helped him find hummingbird nests.

Though a different language proved a challenge, John soon communicated with the Incas.

In the highlands, John filmed llamas. When he climbed above 9,000 feet, he found the world's largest hummingbird, the Giant, almost the size of a robin.

At 13,500 feet, he filmed the world's rarest hummingbird, the Andean Hillstar, which typically feeds while resting rather than hovering.

When John filmed his first Sword-billed Hummingbird, he wrote:

> "The bird looks fantastic with his 12 cm bill and 10 cm body."

John and Dr. Ortiz believed it to be the first time the Sword-billed Hummingbird was ever captured by a film camera. *In The Man Who Loved Birds*, the narrator said, "He thought he could hear chimes ringing in his native Belgium where one day he hoped to show the film."

John's talent and passion led him to places and species never filmed. No wonder he is called a "pioneer in nature cinematography."

> Dr. Fernando Ortiz (1942-2001) was an Ecuadorian biologist and naturalist. Educated in the U.S., he returned to Ecuador and became chair of the biology department at Catholic University in Quito. He founded several nature organizations before his untimely death in a boating accident.

23-12-82 With Dr. Ortiz and his family, I went to Quenca 460 km south of Quito. Quenca is on 2,800 m elevation. The trip took about 12 hours through the beautiful Andes Mountains. Dr. Ortiz set me up in Hotel Quenca while he and his family stayed with relatives.

24-12-82 Quenca. I filmed (200 ft.) the Pasaje de Niños (children's parade). This parade (the only one in Ecuador of its kind) of children and domestic animals goes for over two hours and is absolutely beautiful. Even the animals are dressed with all kinds of fruits.

This parade can be seen every day for seven days as the procession walks from one church to another but the 24th is the main one.

On December 27, John and Dr. Ortiz went up in the mountains to catch hummingbirds in a mist net. They caught the Rainbow Star Frontlet and a Mountain Velvetbreast. They saw the Sapphire-vented Puffleg, Green-tailed Train Bearer, Shining Sunbeam, Sword-billed Hummingbird and many others.

John recorded information about the Sword-billed Hummingbird. When feeding, the bird extends its tongue beyond its bill. When it perches, its beak is nearly vertical with its body to reduce the strain on its neck.

31-12-82 Quenca. Dr. Ortiz, Hernan Loyola (Chief Forester) and I went up in the mountains around Quenca to catch hummingbirds in a mist net (8x22.5m). I filmed them as they caught two hummingbirds, the Sapphire-vented Puffleg and the Tyrian Metaltail. They put them in a specially made harness and weighed them (approximately 6 grams). They fed them with sugar water and released them after the measurement were taken.

3-1-83 Quito. Between San Antonio and Catacali, I saw four Colibris (violet-ears) feeding on the giant century flower which blooms only once in its lifetime (approximately 25 years) and grows to seven meters high. The birds seem to have their territory. Also the Sparkling Violetear and the Black-tailed Train Bearer feeds from this flower. There are many of this plant in the area but only a few with flowers.

21-1-83 I travelled to Hacienda Alexandra located in the lowlands (4.5 hours by bus from Quito) where Johan and Clara Zward run a palm plantage. I filmed the Acestrura Bombus (Woodstar family).

1-2-83 Travelled to La Avelina (70km) where I was introduced to Fritz Cord and Reinhart Sherer, Dutch and German respectively. Close to Volcan Cotopaxi, I filmed the Giant Hummingbird feeding on flowers.

9-2-83 During this trip I filmed lots of the Andean scenery – llamas, Indians, etc.

The Indians liked to be paid a little – 20 cents to a dollar – depending on the circumstances.

13-2-83 La Avelina - Cotopaxi. I went up to Finca Ilitio where I filmed the Giant and the Sword-billed Hummingbirds. Of the latter, I saw two individuals; one was remarkably smaller than the other. Max, the man who rents this farm told me that last November when he was taking the straw roof from a hut; this Sword-billed Hummer was hanging in front of him. Inside he found the nest with two young ones in it. He decided to wait with the roof until the young ones have left the nest. At this moment there is no record of a nest of this species in the world. (South America).

22-2-83 Most of the time the top of the Cotopaxi is covered with clouds. The best time to see the whole mountain is in the morning and sometimes late afternoon.

13-3-83 Returned from Quito to La Avelina and went up in the mountains. I found five nests of the Sparkling Violet Ear. All nests were low in a ravine with the nests in some brush hanging over a vertical wall.

I filmed the Sparkling Violet Ear, the Black-tailed Train Bearer and the Spinning Sunbeam.

From this farm on a clear day, one can see three volcanoes with the highest one Chimborazo at over 6000 meters… I also filmed the second largest hummingbird, the Great Sapphire Wing feeding on the puya flowers from the Bromelia family.

27-3-82 I travelled back to La Avelina and went up in the mountains again for seven days, staying at Finca Ilitio. The red flowers on which the Sword-billed Hummers feed were gone now and I did not see any at all. I filmed for three days on and around the nest of the Sparkling Violetear feeding two young ones in the nest.

This female was not as shy as the previous one filmed on a nest, so I could film this family only 1.5m away without the blind or extension cable.

Many times this female was filmed feeding on Puya flowers.

From the five nests of Sparkling Violetear I found in this ravine, two were molested; the other three had young ones in the nest.

6-4-83 I visited a church near La Avelina where in the past a miracle happened. The tree where Christ appeared was brought into this church. They believe when you visit this church, you are protected against accidents.

> 12-4-83 Tena in the Oriente (jungle). I stayed with the Wadhams for 13 days (Phil is a priest for the Anglican church) and went on a river trip for four days visiting Indian villages along the river… We visited five villages along the river "Rio Napo" which is one of the headwaters of the mighty Amazon River.
>
> In every village we were welcomed by the tribe (everybody shakes hands, also children) and a chicken was slaughtered to make soup for us, something they do not have many times themselves. Also the priests served a mass for the village people and afterwards there was a meeting to discuss the possibility of improving life for the tribes (in two languages because the older people speak only Quichuwa)…
>
> Above Coca the Indians told us there were catfish in the river weighing up to 200 pounds.
>
> Sleeping conditions in the villages were very poor, on a wooden floor with a sleeping bag and the company of the croatches. I was previously bitten by chiggers and it was very difficult to sleep on these pests in tropical heat. The children in the villages looked ill and had swollen stomachs (worms).
>
> On the last day I had cramps in my stomach and also diarrhea. (I learned later in Canada that I had Amoebas). My appetite was low. A McDonald's hamburger would have been a nice treat…

As John traveled throughout Ecuador, he produced many rolls of footage and visited major attractions. On the four-day river trip, villagers allowed him to film them and some of the footage can be seen in his films.

Ecuador Bird List:

- Azara's Spinetail
- Band-tailed Pigeon
- Black-tailed Train Bearer Hummingbird
- Coal-black Flower Piercer
- Great Sapphire Wing Hummingbird
- Great Thrush
- Green-tailed Train Bearer Hummingbird
- Mountain Velvetbreast Hummingbird
- Rainbow Star Frontlet Hummingbird
- Rufous-colored Sparrow

Sapphire-vented Puffleg Hummingbird
Scarlet-bellied Mountain-Tanager
Shining sunbeam Hummingbird
Sparkling Violet-ear Hummingbird
Sword-billed Hummingbird
Tawny Antpitta
Tyrian Metaltail Hummingbird

20-7-83 Toronto - Met with Ralph Ellis and Bob Bocking. We viewed the Grebe footage from Manitoba. Ralph showed a one-hour special from the Galapagos taken from four one-half-hour shows. Afterward, Bob and I viewed the South American Hummingbird footage. Ralph offered me four one-half-hour shows for a new TV series, "Profiles of Nature" for $7500 down and 20% royalties for a 10-year minimum for each show. As of that one-hour special, he offered a 50% deal to be discussed later.

Also received a check from Bob for Great Horned Owl footage used in the "Lorne Greene's New Wilderness" series.

Bonaire, Netherland Antilles, 1984

"I love to fish so this was a dream come true." John Bax

John flew to Curacao, a small island off the coast of Venezuela. From there, he flew into the national park that was to be his home in Bonaire.

John met a priest, Father Candidus, who took him to a house on the beach where he could stay. Although the beach was public, John saw no other people. In this quiet and serene corner of the world, he fished, filmed, and drank in the beauty of each day. Bonaire proved to be one of the most pleasant locations he visited.

He experienced everyone's idea of a true Caribbean lifestyle. He lived close to nature. He dressed in shorts and spent much of his day in the water.

"I did a lot of snorkeling and fishing by hand. One day in the water, I hit up against something, which caused a terrible rash. I itched for days," John said.

The Washington Slagbaai National Park, the Netherland Antilles' first nature sanctuary, is located on the northwest side of Bonaire. It was here that John filmed the Greater Flamingos working their way through the shallow waters.

22-10-83 Landed in Kralendyk at 9:00pm.

24-10-83 Visited Police Office to pick up my passport and asked for visa for six months. I have to come back on 4-11-83.

25-10-83 Kralendyk – saw Tropical Mockingbird, Ruby-topaz Hummingbird, Grove-billed Ani, Caribbean Parakeet and Killdeer.

26-10-83 Saw Black-winged Stilt, Brown Pelican, Lesser Yellowlegs, Greater Yellowlegs, Northern Waterthrush. Visited the salt factory and saw the slave huts.

27-10-83 Moved to Washington National Park (WNP) and I had filmed some birds feeding on cactus fruit.

28-10-83 Saw Greater Flamingos and nests of the Yellow Oriole, Tricolored Heron, Snowy Egret, Oystercatcher, Osprey, Brown Pelican, Ruddy Turnstone, Yellow Warbler, Great Blue Heron, Neotropic Cormorant, Green Heron, lots of lizards and iguanas. Filmed Stilt Sandpiper, iguana, Greater Flamingo.

4-11-83 Travelled back to Kralendyk as I ran out of food and water. Visited Police Office and have to come back on 21-11-83.

6-11-83 Did some more fishing but cannot catch any big ones.

10-11-83 WNP. I waved a small fishing boat to shore and bought a barracuda. The two men did not want anything for it but I gave them two gulden. Taste was good (fried in butter).

11-11-83 Saw Blue Grosbeak – new bird for the island of Bonaire.

14-11-83 Kralendyk. I caught a yellowtail fish with live bait. With Father Candidus, I came back to WNP to identify the Blue Grosbeak. He took several pictures of this female since it was new to Bonaire.

I see the Blue Grosbeak around the house in Slagbaai regularly.

15-11-83 WNP. Found nest of Bananaquit with young ones in the nest. Nest was located in cactus plant about 1.3m high. Saw mating of Crested Caracara. The male approached the female from the air. It flew on top of the female and mating took place.

6-12-83 Kralendyk. Took in the three forms for the six-month visa.

17-12-83 WNP. Finally filmed the Osprey at 48 fps as it landed on top of pipe cactus. Took me five days of 3.5 hours each to take this shot. Today they will catch goats in the park and sell the live animals for three gulden ($2.10) per Kg.

20-12-83 I went to Kralendyk and back to the Park. I visited Verjilio in Rincon. He caught a swordfish of 70 Kg a few days earlier. Frater Candidus drove me back to the park. I paid him $14 for gas.

22-12-83 WNP. Did some fishing with the snorkel in the morning. In the afternoon I went fishing with Cecilio, a local fisherman. We fished until 10:30pm. I caught five fish and lost two barracudas.

****

John discovered two Brown Pelicans that needed his help. Unable to care for themselves, John hand fed them, carried them into the water, and worked with them until they learned to fish on their own.

He filmed White Pelicans, Whooping Cranes, Greater Flamingos, Black-winged Stilts, and a Gila monster. He discovered a couple of new hummingbird species — the Black-tailed Train Bearer and the Ruby-topaz Hummingbirds. He would see the Black-tailed Train Bearers again in Central America, but he never saw the Ruby-topaz anywhere else.

John discovered eleven Ruby-topaz nests. He filmed them day after day. The birds loved the flowers on the aloe plants. With his affinity for birds, the hummingbirds gradually accepted his close presence. "I offered one of them a spoonful of nectar. It took a lot of quiet and patience but finally the bird ate from the spoon," he said.

He noted that the male never helped with the nesting responsibilities. The female took care of the young and the nest while the male sat preening a short distance away.

24-2-83 Walked up to Playa Frans and found nests of Yellow Warbler with three eggs. Bananaquit with three eggs and other nest with two young in the nest. Saw lots of white flowers on which both species of hummingbird – Ruby-topaz and Common Emerald – are feeding. The cactus has yellow flowers. A few Aloe plants are starting to bloom. In the afternoon Miguel took me to

Rincon where I stayed until 26-12.

21-1-84 WNP. Ruby-topaz Hummingbird. Saw ♀ on nest three times… Saw Pearly-eyed Thrasher. Ruby-topaz Hummingbird nest #2 ♀ came on nest with me standing less than 1m away.

In the afternoon, I filmed the ♀ from nest #2. I was able to touch the bird on the nest several times.

22-1-84 WNP. Filmed nest #2 again touching the female on the nest. First I pointed at nest, then in close up, then I hold finger beside nest to show how small nest is. Filmed close up with female landing on nest several times.

23-1-84 WNP. Filmed nest #2, the female on the nest taking sugar water from me in a teaspoon several times and with different shirts on to make it looks like I was doing this on separate days.

24-1-84 WNP. I visited nest #2 and fed the female sugar water with a teaspoon. Also visited nest #4 and noticed that the nest was built up more.

I filmed nest #2 again (with 10mm lens) feeding sugar water to the female while she incubated two eggs. The camera was only 40cm from the nest.

Over the next couple of months, John documented when each egg hatched and the care the mother gave her young. On many days he was only 20-30cm from the nest as he filmed the feeding of the young. It took around fourteen days for most of the eggs to hatch.

John stayed on Bonaire for three months in 1984 after his Ecuador adventure. It remained one of his favorite trips.

Bonaire Bird list:

American Oystercatcher
Bananaquit
Bare-eyed Pigeon
Belted Kingfisher
Black-faced Grasquit
Blackpoll Warbler
Black-tailed Train Bearer Hummingbird
Black-whiskered Vireo
Black-winged Stilt
Blue Grosbeak – new bird for Bonaire

Brown Booby
Brown Pelican
Brown-crested Flycatcher
Caribbean Elaenia
Caribbean Parakeet
Common Emerald Hummingbird
Crested Caracara
Eared Dove
Gray Kingbird
Gray Plover
Great Blue Heron
Great White Egret
Greater Flamingo
Greater Yellowleg
Green Heron
Groove-billed Ani
Ground Dove
Killdeer
Least Sandpiper
Least Tern
Lesser Yellowleg
Magnificent Frigatebird
Mangrove Cuckoo
Merlin
Neotropic Cormorant
Northern Waterthrush
Osprey
Pearly-eyed Thrasher
Peregrine Falcon
Reddish Egret
Red-necked Pigeon
Ruby-topaz Hummingbird
Ruddy Turnstone
Sanderling
Semi-palmated Plover
Semi-palmated Sandpiper
Short-billed Dowitcher
Smooth Flycatcher
Snowy Egret
Snowy Plover
Stilt Sandpiper
Thick-billed Plover

Tri-colored Heron
Tropical Mockingbird
Whimbrel
White Pelican
White-cheeked Pintail
White-tailed Hawk
White-tipped Dove
Whooping Crane
Willet
Yellow Oriole
Yellow Warbler
Yellow-billed Cuckoo
Yellow-crowned Night Heron
Yellow-shouldered Parrot

Rio Grande Valley, 1985

"South Texas is a wonderful place to find birds." John Bax

John first visited the Rio Grande Valley in south Texas in 1984. He stayed five months and fell in love with the area.

8-10-84 Left London Ontario for Big Bend National Park where I arrived on 11-10-84.

14-10-84 Visited South Padre Island. Birds: Long-billed Curlew, Black-necked Stilt and Wood Ibis.

15-10- 84 Visited Santa Ana Refuge. Birds: Fulvous Whistling Duck, Least Grebe.

John spent most of his days at Laguna Atascosa National Wildlife Refuge or at Santa Ana National Wildlife Refuge. He filmed whenever he could find the right location and kept detailed notes of his film footage. Laguna Atascosa combines coastal wetlands, marshes and semi-desert lands.

Day after day, he spent from dawn till dusk sitting in a blind waiting for the perfect shot. He was rewarded with infrequent but spectacular opportunities to capture bird behavior.

12-2-85 Visited Laguna Atascosa Refuge. Filmed 2 Alligators. One was eating a duck, also filmed on the same pond Lesser

Scaup, Blue-winged Teal and Least Grebes. Mailed out 14x100 foot of 7252 film.

23-2-85 Rio Hondo. Filmed: About 500 Black-bellied Whistling Ducks in slow motion

12-3-85 Laguna Atascosa Refuge. Filmed: Harold and Ruth Burgess as they checked and cleaned the bird boxes for the Black-bellied Whistling Ducks. Quite a few of the boxes were occupied by Barn Owls.

Box #1: Barn Owl flew out of nest box. There were 4 eggs in it.

In 2 other boxes Barn Owls flew out (sometimes there were 2 adults) but no contents.

Box #2: Barn Owl flew out, 3 eggs in it.

Also filmed alligator.

20-3-85 Laguna Atascosa. Filmed: Barn Owl leaving nest box #2 on 64 frames per second. There were only 2 eggs in nest (previously 3).

Box #1 – 5 eggs in box but they were cold (abandoned).

17-4-85 to 21-4-85 Laguna Atascosa. Filmed: Richard Ward as he checked 18 animal traps every morning with a live chicken in each trap.

Richard Ward was a graduate student from the University of British Columbia. Filmed as he works with raccoon and opossum, which were trapped. He takes blood samples, weighs the animal, collects fleas and ticks, examines and measures teeth, measures the overall length of the animal, and measures the ears and length of tail.

John left for Canada on May 22, 1985. He had completely filled his journal that started back in 1975.

(Author's Note: When I visited Cornell's Laboratory of Ornithology to view John's notes and raw film footage, I did not find any other journals. He gave me a copy of the notes from his 1995 trip to Belgium, part of a journal from his Bonaire trip and a note from his visit to Jamaica.)

Every year in South Texas, John filmed at Laguna Atascosa National Wildlife Refuge near Port Isabel and South Padre Island. It is the southernmost waterfowl refuge in the United States.

These films became part of the documentary, *Journey to Brazoria*, which covered Laguna Atascosa and the Brazoria National Wildlife Refuge near Freeport, TX.

Birds on South Texas trip

Altamira Oriole
American Coot
Barn Owl
Black Skimmer
Black-bellied Whistling Duck
Black-crested Titmouse
Black-necked Stilt
Blue-winged Teal
Boat-tailed Grackle
Common Egret
Double-crested Cormorant
Eastern Screech Owl
Forster's Tern
Fulvous Whistling Duck
Golden-fronted Woodpecker
Great Blue Heron
Green Jay
Gull-billed Tern
Ladder-backed Woodpecker
Least Grebe
Lesser Scaup
Long-billed Curlew
Pied-billed Grebe
Plain Chachalaca
Red-billed Pigeon
Scissor-tailed Flycatcher
Vermilion Flycatcher
White Ibis
White Pelican
White-faced Ibis
White-tipped Dove
Wild Turkey
Willet
Wilson's Plover
Wood Ibis

Animals:

- Alligator
- Bobcat
- Jaguarundi
- Javelina
- Mexican Ground Squirrel
- Nutria (large semi-aquatic rodent)
- Ocelot
- Opossum
- Raccoon
- Rattlesnake

After traveling south for several years, John moved to the Rio Grande Valley where he remained a full-time resident. He spent the last twenty-five-plus years filming in the southern US, Mexico, and Central America.

As he worked around the Valley, he met ranchers and ranch managers who allowed him access to their properties.

Seney National Wildlife Refuge, Upper Michigan, 1987

John went to Seney in search of Yellow Rails. It turned out to be one of the few trips that met with little filming success but proved to be an adventurous experience.

As he searched for the birds, he had to break open beaver dams to get through the marsh.

The first day right after he parked his trailer, he left his camp and headed out on foot in search of birds. He walked through the marshes most of the day searching for nests. When evening arrived, he realized he was lost. He walked most of the night, fighting off the mosquitoes. He tried to lay down to rest occasionally but it was extremely cold. He got up and walked again.

He didn't find the camp until the next day. He must have walked in circles much of the night. John always remembered the overwhelming relief when he found his camp that day. He wrote about it in a letter to Alice and she sensed both his fear and his relief.

He filmed much less than on other trips and ended the month realizing he didn't have enough good footage to sell.

****

Seney National Wildlife Refuge, established in 1935, consists of more than 95,000 acres that provides habitat for resident wildlife and migratory birds. Created from swamps left by glaciers, it is located in Michigan's Upper Peninsula.

Arizona, 1989

"Madera Canyon is a filmmaker's dream." John Bax

"I've been around birds all my life and hummingbirds fascinate me the most. I went to Arizona to find the hummingbirds."

John found them. He parked his trailer at the Santa Rita research camp near Madera Canyon, put out all of his hummingbird feeders and waited.

To feed them, he mixed four parts of boiled water to one part granulated sugar. He never used red food coloring because it can cause tumors on the bird's tongue.

Madera Canyon is home to eighteen species of hummingbirds. John not only filmed them, he gained their trust. Mornings started with John sitting near the feeders. He used two cameras, operating both by remote control.

He loved experimenting with the birds – always trying to get them to come closer. In Madera Canyon, a hummingbird perched on his finger and another time, drank from a feeder John held in his mouth.

For the first time in fifty years, John saw a Phainopepla (from the Silky Flycatcher family). He caught a feeding session of two chicks.

John's work resulted in a one-hour TV special entitled *The Treasure of Madera Canyon*, produced by KEG Productions in association with CF-CN-TV Calgary, the Global Television Network, and The Family Channel.

Madera Canyon is home to 150 species of nesting and migratory birds including the Blue Grosbeak, the Vermillion Flycatcher, Western Tanager, the Magnificent Hummingbird, and the Elegant Trogon. John successfully captured many different species on film.

Birds Filmed:

Acorn Woodpecker
Anna's Hummingbird
Ash-throated Flycatcher
Black-chinned Hummingbird
Black-headed Grosbeak
Black-throated Gray Warbler
Blue Grosbeak
Blue-throated Hummingbird
Bridled Titmouse

Broad-billed Hummingbird
Broad-tailed Hummingbird
Brown-crested Flycatcher
Bullock's Oriole
Cactus Wren
Calliope Hummingbird
Chipping Sparrow
Cooper's Hawk
Costa's Hummingbird
Dusky-capped Flycatcher
Elegant Trogon
Elf Owl
Flamulated Owl
Gambel's Quail
Gray-breasted Jay (aka Mexican Jay)
House Finch
Lazuli Bunting
Lesser Goldfinch
Lucy's Warbler
Magnificent Hummingbird
Mourning Dove
Northern or Bullock's Oriole
Painted Redstart
Phainopepla
Rufous Hummingbird
Scott's Oriole
Strickland's Woodpecker
Sulphur-bellied Flycatcher
Turkey Vulture
Vermillion Flycatcher
Western Kingbird
Western Screech Owl
Western Tanager
Whiskered Screech Owl
White-breasted Nuthatch
White-crowned Sparrow
White-winged Dove
Wilson's Warbler
Yellow-breasted Chat
Yellow-eyed Junco

Animals filmed:

- Apache Fox Squirrel
- Arizona Gray Squirrel
- Coatimundi (relative of raccoon)
- Desert Cottontail Rabbit
- Harris's Antelope Squirrel
- Ingrid's Tassel-eared Squirrel
- Javelina
- Lizard
- Mule Deer
- Rock Squirrel
- Short Horned Lizard
- Tree Lizard
- White-tailed Deer

Chapter 8: The 1990s

Brazoria National Wildlife Refuge, Texas, 1990

"I loved the solitude and the diversity." John Bax

Over the years that John filmed the birds of the Rio Grande Valley, he talked with many birders. He listened to stories and comments about the birding at a place called the Brazoria National Wildlife Refuge south of Houston. Several told him that he would find five species of rails in the refuge.

"I had never seen a film on rails so I decided to go there and film them," John said. He found that the refuge is home to 270 resident and/or migratory bird species as well as alligators, snakes, red-eared turtles, green anoles (the only native anole found in the United States), armadillos, and other wildlife.

Since the refuge is not open to the public, he had to apply for a special permit. He set up his trailer in the refuge and lived there for three-and-a-half months. He had the refuge to himself — an ideal condition for finding nests, observing behavior and filming.

A journalist from the area visited him. He showed her around the refuge. He showed her an alligator. When they went to look, it came out of the water after her. John kept wondering why. He went back and found a nest. He decided to film it. He set up his stuff and got someone to run the camera for him. The alligator came out of the water after him. He showed himself running away.

John used two cameras, many times setting one up to film himself as he searched for nests. He operated the cameras by remote control. In some cases, the camera was within inches of a nest.

He typically used a blind but some birds allowed him to film them without the blind. In the film, John is shown sitting under a sun umbrella while filming by remote control.

He found fifteen nests of Least Bitterns and he filmed two. In the film, he noted the unpleasant conditions — insects and heat. He described sitting in the blind in just his shorts with sweat dripping down and insects, particularly mosquitoes, driving him nuts. "I think I'm crazy to do these things," he quipped.

Birds Filmed in Brazoria:

- Black Vulture
- Black-necked Stilt
- Clapper Rail
- Common Moorhen
- Common Nighthawk
- Eastern Kingbird
- King Rail
- Least Bittern
- Purple Gallinule
- Ruddy Turnstone
- Turkey Vulture
- Wilson's Plover

The resulting film, *Journey to Brazoria: A Bird Safari with John Bax*, was produced by KEG Productions in 1990, and became a Profiles in Nature special. The documentary includes his work in both the Laguna Atascosa Wildlife Refuge and the Brazoria National Wildlife Refuge.

John and the Gorgas Science Foundation

"They are doing wonderful things for nature. Working with them challenged me to always do better." John Bax

An artist friend, Tony Bennett contacted the Gorgas Science Foundation and suggested they introduce themselves to John's work.

Richard Moore, a South Texas photographer, writer and owner of Valley Nature Film Productions, and his brother Pete Moore introduced John to the Cielito Reserve and told Larry Lof, director of the Gorgas Science Foundation, that he should make a film with John.

Bob Bocking, who John originally knew from KEG Productions, worked as John's agent and editor. These connections all came together and over the next few years, the Gorgas Science Foundation produced a number of documentaries with John's films.

> The Gorgas Science Foundation, Inc. (www.gsfinc.org) is a nonprofit organization affiliated with the University of Texas Brownsville and Texas Southmost College. Their mission is to promote conservation through education.

Through the Gorgas Science Foundation, John filmed in Mexico and Texas. He provided the film footage for four Gorgas productions.

John's life and career are highlighted in two films: *The Man Who Loved*

Birds produced by KEG Productions in 1986, and *A Passion for Birds* by the Gorgas Science Foundation in 1996.

El Cielito, Mexico, 1991

Eastern escarpment of Sierra Madre Oriental

El Cielito is a biology field station at the foot of the eastern escarpment of the Sierra Madre Mountains in northeastern Mexico.

In 1965, the Gorgas Science Foundation and Texas Southmost College set up a biology field station at Rancho del Cielo. Gorgas purchased Rancho del Cielito in 1983 to preserve hundreds of acres and nearly a mile of fast disappearing ecosystems along the Rio Sabinas.

Eventually the State of Tamaulipas created the 360,000-acre El Cielo Biosphere Reserve.

John traveled to El Cielito to produce the camera work for a film entitled At a Bend in a Mexican River.

He experienced 116-degree temperatures that didn't abate at night. Sleep was nearly impossible in the heat. John soaked his sheets in cold water before he went to bed.

He stayed in a house owned by the university with an American caretaker named Juanita. The university supplied the food but he only saw students when they visited. Although the university had two trucks, John walked everywhere. The students used the trucks for their work.

John found lots of trouble. Dense plant life covered the poison ivy and poison oak. The clean river water was good for bathing and swimming. However, one time he accidentally laid his towel in poison oak. His rash covered his entire body. He was so sick that his companions feared he wouldn't survive. Juanita, who had been a nurse, took care of him.

> Juanita Coalson, an American citizen from Arkansas, fell in love with Mexico. When John visited El Cielito, he met Juanita, who was working for the Gorgas Science Foundation as a caretaker in the reserve.
>
> John and Alice appreciated the kindness and care she showed toward John on numerous occasions. Juanita celebrated her 100th birthday in Harlingen, Texas. Soon after that, she moved back to Mexico, where she died in April of 2010, at the age of 103.

He suffered several rashes while there. Once in the jungle he used a machete to cut through the entangled vines. A huge wasp attacked him. Juanita gave him medicine to alleviate the swelling and pain.

Brazil, 1991/1992

John read about the late Dr. Augusto Ruschi, the hummingbird man from Brazil. He contacted the refuge that Dr. Ruschi had started and they invited him to Brazil. They provided a home for him.

"I put out so many hummingbird feeders that we had to fill them every hour." John smiled at that memory. His eyes lit when he talked about surrounding himself with feeders.

Alice accompanied him and helped keep the feeders full. She learned ways she could assist him with his equipment and notes. She described herself as the "chief cook & bottle washer." She found time to read and knit, two activities she enjoys.

"When we went to town, the birds would be waiting for us when we returned. They surrounded John and let him know they were still hungry," Alice remembered.

"When I first agreed to help John film, I had no idea that I would end up in such ridiculous situations…holding his lamp in awkwarvd positions… moving in and out of forests and marshes. It was an adventure," Alice laughed at the telling.

John filmed many species of hummingbirds including nesting birds. It was a rainy season and he experienced a lot of difficulty finding nests.

He put bananas on the porch. The first day, two little colorful birds came and often revisited them. Alice believed they knew John Bax was there to take their pictures.

"I found it difficult to keep up with John, and here I was, eleven years younger," Alice admitted. After a long day in the field, Alice came home exhausted.

> Augusto Ruschi was a renowned hummingbird scholar from Brazil. In addition to his many works, he founded the Augusto Ruschi Biological Reserve in the Atlantic Forest Mountains near Santa Teresa, Brazil.
>
> In one of his writings, he described the courting dance of hummingbirds:
>
> "The male flies in circles very near the female, above and around her, chirping low as she watches him, turning her head to follow his movements. He approaches more closely and opening his bill sticks out his tongue and lets it drop in an exquisite and ridiculous manner…. until the female at last gives signs of potential surrender."

"A friend once remarked, 'John's just not normal,'" Alice laughed. "That's what we all felt like when we tried to keep up with him."

The cabin was in the woods. Not far away, a small river flowed. They could walk along the river to Dr. Ruschi's grave. In the town, there was a small hummingbird museum.

"We went one time to film a rare hummingbird that had been rescued. John filmed it because it was so rare. He didn't like filming birds in captivity," Alice said.

Based on John's filming success, Tony Mercieca visited and photographed birds in the same area of Brazil.

John spent three months filming in Brazil. His one disappointment in his career was that the footage from Brazil was never used in a film. It nagged at him and was the stimulus to contact Cornell University. He died with the confidence that they would eventually use it.

El Cielo, Mexico, 1992

"I must have walked three hundred miles." John Bax

El Cielo is home to America's northernmost tropical cloud forests located along the eastern escarpment of northeastern Mexico's Sierra Madre. Eight separate eco-systems flourish there. The area's exceptional diversity provides habitat for many species of wildlife. It is home to tropical jungles, mountain forests, pine-oak forests and dwarf oak and heath forests.

The living conditions were primitive. John considered the lack of modern conveniences a challenge. Alice missed them. She heated a rock to keep warm at night.

"It was kind of difficult," John said. However, he was awestruck by the beauty. He loved being up in the clouds every day and thoroughly enjoyed his work there.

There was no vehicle but there was a pack mule to carry supplies. With a guide and a pack mule, John searched for the Bumblebee Hummingbird. They saw few people as they traveled and only occasionally passed a homestead.

When they reached their destination, John and his guide settled into a cabin. Within a few minutes the first Bumblebee Hummingbird appeared. The gorgeous colors of the bird, one of the smallest in the world, brightened the forest.

Their nests were so small that they were barely visible.

The next morning, they loaded up their gear and went in search of more. John's footage of the hummingbirds they found clearly demonstrated his love for them.

He also went in search of Macaws. He pitched a blind at the edge of a 300-foot cliff and waited for days before finding a pair of Macaws. He captured them on film.

"Ah, I think it's time to quit," John said after the months of climbing uphill through dense brush and forest. However, he filmed for the remaining nineteen years of his life. He did buy a video camera that drastically cut the weight that he had to carry around.

The cloud forest, halfway up the escarpment, is bathed in heavy mist. In the film, John said that the nesting failure rate is high, requiring continuous nesting.

Alice's son and his future wife, James and Leslie, visited them. One day they all went for a walk and got lost. Turned around, they ended up on the other side of the mountain. They walked into a refuge and John couldn't believe where he was. All he could say was, "How could that be?"

John and Alice decided to walk into town (a 3-hour journey) for the night. John advised James to go on ahead to the road to get back to camp. Alice's knee gave out and she experienced pain the entire way. She was also worried about a deadly snake, the fer-de-lance that lives in El Cielo. When they reached the road, John didn't follow his own advice and went in the opposite direction.

"John wouldn't give up. He showed the same persistence and determination that characterized everything he did," Alice said.

By the time John and Alice reached town, they were soaking wet. They found a woman who gave them one towel and told them she had a bed in the barn. Freezing cold and wet, they shared the towel and headed for the barn. They found a little bed – hardly big enough for one person. Exhaustion led to sleep.

"The next thing we remembered was a donkey braying and a rooster crowing." They walked back to their

> The fer-de-lance is the most dangerous of Mexico's snakes and its bite is usually fatal. It is an aggressive, nocturnal viper that can be found almost anywhere – in a tree, on the jungle floor, in the grass or out in the open. Its markings are not distinct, so it is hard to identify. It has an arrow-shaped head and a mouth with two retractable fangs appearing too big for the snake's head.
>
> http://www.mexicotravelvacations.com/article/492/Mexican-Animal-Life-Snakes-Mexico-vacation-help/

house and found her son out looking for them. The truck that had been sent for them got stuck in the mud.

"It made James nervous," said Alice. She wasn't at all worried. Months later, when John and Alice decided to marry, they called James to tell him.

"After our escapade in Mexico, I wasn't sure you'd be okay with me marrying your mother," John told James.

James told his mother it was her life and anything she wanted to do was fine with him.

It was one of the adventures that John would rather not talk about.

John was there for four months. The rainy season runs from June to October, accounting for most of the ten feet of rainfall per year.

He filmed a sequence of a squirrel eating Mountain Trogon eggs. There is a segment about the mites that live on hummingbirds in the El Cielo film. He listened to the Barred Antshrikes that vibrate their tails while they're singing.

The highlight of John's expedition was the filming of the Bumblebee Hummingbird, which is just two-and-a-half inches from the tip of its tail to the tip of its bill. He also filmed the White-eared Hummingbird.

John's filming portrayed the exquisite beauty of the rain forest. With his two-camera filming, viewers watched him as he searched for birds and their nests.

Birds filmed:

Amazon Kingfisher
Barred Antshrike
Bronze-winged Woodpecker
Bumblebee Hummingbird
Common Potoo
Curassow
Hooded Grosbeak
Military Macaw
Motmot
Mountain Trogon
Ringed Kingfisher
Rufous-capped Thrush Finch
White-eared Hummingbird

Texas, 1993/1994

"I have a special love for the Rio Grande Valley and especially Laguna Atascosa National Wildlife Refuge." John Bax

John spent all of 1993 and 1994 filming in Texas for the *Treasures of the Rio Grande Delta* film. He focused on the birds, butterflies, plants, flowers and history of the area.

He explored the entire area and learned about the region's various habitats. He filmed animals and particularly enjoyed studying the nesting habits of the alligators.

By the time he finished, he had three years of film on the Valley. The resulting program became one of John's most popular works.

The longer he stayed, the more he loved the entire Rio Grande Valley. "The birds came to me," he said. "They love it here, too. You can find great diversity and perfect habitat. I recommend that everybody come to the Valley."

Over the years, John developed close relationships with several photographers in the Valley. They spent countless hours with John, riding the back roads looking for birds and nests.

Photographer Steve Sinclair, in a recent article in the *Coastal Current*, said:

"John had an incredible ability to instantly size up habitat to tell if a certain bird would be there."

Steve acknowledged that if John said a bird would be there, "you could take it to the bank."

Belgium, 1995

"I was honored by the invitation from the Wielewaal." John Bax

John had made many trips home to Belgium, while working for Philips. He also went for KEG Production's filming of *The Man Who Loved Birds*, which was released in 1986.

John received a welcome by the mayor. He had lunch with dignitaries from the city, the *Wielewaal*, an old teacher, and his brother, Leo.

In the documentary, *The Man Who Loved Birds*, he said, "There in the setting of my old schoolyard, with people I had known since youth, I was carried back almost fifty years, and I could see myself clearly at the age of ten...always the first one out when the school bell rang...out of the door and off and running...

"Then away again, over some trenches, still faintly visible from the First World War. And finally…the nest of the Crested Grebe.

"I would sit there by the hour, dreaming ahead to the places I would go, and the birds that I would see when I was a grown up and in full charge of my own life."

In 1995, John presented his film, *Treasures of the Rio Grande Delta*, at a 600-seat theater in his hometown of Turnhout. Whiles there, he grabbed the opportunity to film birds he hadn't seen since his youth.

Alice remembers standing on the corner across from the church where John married Elizabeth. He filmed the church and the flags that adorned the streets. The flags represented playing cards, for which the city of Turnhout is famous.

"We worked on filming the nest of the Black Woodpecker," Alice said. She watched as John filmed the bird chipping away at the wood. She gathered the wood chippings and dropped them so John could film them falling to the ground. When he filmed the Mute Swan, it took after Alice. "I was afraid of it. It came out of the water and chased me every time I came near."

They filmed the Crested Grebe in a park. Alice was able to get close to the bird while John filmed it.

At the film showing, the *Wielewaal*, the Oriole Society, presented John with an honorary lifetime membership.

John and Alice arrived in Turnhout on March 21, 1995, and flew back to Texas one month later.

In an interview in Turnhout, a reporter asked John if his passion for birds began in his childhood.

"Indeed," John replied, "Birds attracted me as a child. I experienced the pioneering days of the Wielewaal, which was founded by Father Segers. Also, Willem Paulussen, the former director of the school of Zevendonk, was there… Did you know that this year Paulussen's book, *The Breeding Birds of the Kempen*, appeared in English? An English publisher brought the book to market with its beautiful illustrations."

The following selected journal excerpts give a glimpse of John's thrill to have the equipment to film the birds he studied in his childhood. Surely he thought back to the first borrowed binoculars and his earliest desires to capture the beauty he discovered.

25-3-95. Film presentations at 8:00pm and 9:30pm in the

"Heischuur" for the Wielewaal. I presented: "Treasures of the Rio Grande Delta."

29-3-95. Filmed: The Black Woodpecker cleaning out a nest hole in a beuk about 5 meters high. Male and female took turns in cleaning out the nest hole. Used zoom, 230MM lens. Location: Between Baarle and Weelde Statie.

Filmed on a pond: Swan, Tufted Duck, Mallard. Saw two nests of Crested Grebes only 7-8 meters apart… It was cold -1 to +5c.

1-4-95. Long-tailed Tit. Filmed pair as they were nest building in Christmas tree about 1.5 meter high. Used 10mm-zoom lens and 230 mm Lens.

Tawny Owl. Filmed on two nest boxes. Me climbing tree to nest box. Owl flies out of the nest box. I show the egg I took for nest box (4 eggs in nest). Climbing down from nest tree. On second nest box, owl flies out. I climbing up to nest box and show young one (2 in nest). Climbing down, me looking through binoculars.

12-4-95 Trip to Philips land. Filmed: Brant, Common Shelduck, Oystercatcher, Avocet, 2 Mute Swans on nest, Crested Grebe. Finished roll #7. Trip was done with Rick Otten, Jan Sterckx, Jan Verschuren and myself.

16-4-95 Liereman – Turnhout. Filmed: church. Wielewaal group on an outing in the Liereman. Finished roll #8. Filmed: On and around market place, city hall and Castle of Turnhout. Finished Rolls #9 and 10.

****

John filmed 22 bird species in Belgium with 10 species on nest.

Avocet
Barnacle Goose
Black Woodpecker
Blackbird
Blue Heron colony
Brambling
Brant
Chaf Finch

Cool Tit
Crested Grebe
Crested Tit
Great Tit
Green Finch
Lapwing
Long-tailed Tit
Mute Swan
Oystercatcher
Shelduck
Siskin
Tawny Owl
Tree Sparrow
Tufted Duck

RAINBOW TROUT

JOHN BAX – TEXAS
STEISTEL LAKE
SEPT. 9/00 11.7 LBS.

Chapter 9: Birds of a Feather

"I'm the guy who carried his tripod." Larry Lof

"Everybody loves John. He's so humble," Larry Lof, the Executive Director of the Gorgas Science Foundation, said when I mentioned John. "We made four films with him."

"Did you work with him personally?" I asked.

"I'm the guy who carried his tripod," Larry laughed. "Boy, do I have stories to tell."

Seth Patterson, a nature photographer who works for Gorgas, laughed and agreed that he too had stories about John.

Ultimately, I interviewed Larry and Seth, as well as photographers Steve Sinclair and Lee Zieger. All knew and worked with John for many years. Each spoke of his time with John with affection, admiration, and humor.

Bob Bocking

"I met John Bax while we were both working on the *Audubon Wildlife Theatre* television series produced by Keg Productions in Toronto, Ontario. I was working as a cinematographer as well as an editor on the series in the 1960s. John began filming wildlife, mainly birds, after photographing birds as a still photographer. His early work was difficult to edit because he lacked the experience and equipment needed to develop sequences. I explained the need to film long shots, medium shots and close-ups using different focal length lenses and changing the viewpoint. John learned quickly and his work improved a great deal."

Bob and Urane Bocking

Bob related an incident that occurred when they were filming the show titled *Long Point Marsh*.

"We walked up to our waist in chest waders looking for nests while I filmed John. At one point I stepped into a hole, my waders filled with very cold water, and I couldn't move. John finally was able to pull me out!

"I think what impressed me the most about John was his ability to gain the confidence of many of the birds he filmed. He would film himself right beside a nest while the adult bird was still incubating the eggs. He was able to do this with a remarkable variety of species.

"John would decide to do a show on a single species of bird such as warblers, hummingbirds, and grebes. He travelled all over North, Central, and South America to complete his collection of species.

"Once the *Audubon Wildlife Theatre* series was completed, John began to contribute to a new series of hour-long shows, *Profiles of Nature.* I recall travelling to London, Ontario to film segments for *The Man Who Loved Birds*, setting up a high speed camera to film hummingbirds coming into his trailer while John was sitting there watching it at the feeder. All this in slow motion!"

After John moved to southern Texas, he and Bob kept in touch over the years.

"Larry Lof at the Gorgas Science Foundation and John suggested that we should work together on some films the foundation wanted to sponsor. My wife and I travelled to Texas and Mexico while working on several films. It was a wonderful collaboration resulting in some really good films.

"I recall camped high in the mountains of Mexico on a quest to film the Bumblebee Hummingbird, the world's smallest, as well as the Macaws that were nesting in a canyon. I had never experienced the rain that poured down on that trip. I was recording sound at the time and was able to capture the faint call of the tiny Bumblebee Hummingbird as well as the raucous calls of the macaws.

I consider it a privilege to have known and worked with John over the years. I don't know of anyone with a more patient, respectful and loving attitude toward the wildlife he filmed.

After I retired from the film business, I took up oil painting. John inspired the painting included in this book.

Lawrence "Larry" Lof

"John was a pioneer in nature cinematography. When he started out, he had to film for hours, then find and edit a few seconds of usable film. It's so much easier with digital photography.

"Lighter equipment has also made it easier today."

Photo by Tony Mercieca
Sword-billed Hummingbird
Ecuador

Photo by Tony Mercieca
Great Gray Owls
Saskatchewan

Photo by Tony Mercieca
Sandhill Cranes
Texas

Photo by Seth Patterson
Barn Owl
Rio Grande Valley

Photo by Seth Patterson
Green Parakeets
Rio Grande Valley

Photo by Seth Patterson
Harris's Hawk nest
Rio Grande Valley

Photo by Seth Patterson
Alligator mother and babies
Laguna Atascosa National Wildlife Refuge

Photo by Steve Sinclair
Barn Owl chicks
Rio Grande Valley

John found a nesting Barn Owl in eastern Cameron County and documented the offspring from birth to fledgling. He spent countless hours alone in the darkness to get the right film.

Photo by Steve Sinclair
Mexican Ground Squirrel

Wildlife was as near as the back of his home in Port Isabel for John Bax. He set out a pan with water and food that attracted all kinds of critters that John would film and Steve would photograph. A frequent visitor to his setup was this Mexican ground squirrel that came in for a drink.

Photo by Steve Sinclair
Green Parakeet
Rio Grande Valley

Filming birds in the wild took John Bax to some interesting places, including the University of Texas at Brownsville - Texas Southmost College where he filmed this Green Parakeet.

Photo by Lee Zieger
Red-crowned Parrots
Brownsville, TX

John and Lee made many trips together. Filming parrots was a favorite activity.

Photo by Lee Zieger
Red-lored Parrot

Photo by Lee Zieger
Yellow-headed Parrot

Photo by Lee Zieger
Wild Turkeys
Rio Grande Valley

Photo by Bill Purcell
Black-chinned Hummingbird
Rio Grande Valley

Bill Purcell and John lived at Fun n Sun RV Park at the same time. Bill joined John on the many birding trips.

Photo by Bill Purcell
Broad-tailed Hummingbird
Rio Grande Valley

Photo by Bill Purcell
Broad-billed Hummingbird
Rio Grande Valley

Photo by Bill Purcell
Broad-billed Hummingbird

Photo by Madeleine Sandefur
Keel-billed Toucan
Costa Rica

Photo by Madeleine Sandefur
Magnificent Hummingbird
Costa Rica

John filmed both the Keel-billed Toucan and the Magnificent Hummingbird when he was in Costa Rica.

Photo by Madeline Sandefur
Green Violet-eared Hummingbird
Costa Rica

Photo by George Peck
Common Pauraque Chicks

Photo by George Peck
Plain Chachalaca

Photo by George Peck
White-tailed Kite
Texas

Photo by George Peck
Least Grebe
Texas

Painting by Bob Bocking, Artist
Ruby-throated Hummingbird
"This painting was inspired by John."

John with the 16mm camera he used throughout most of his career.

As the Foundations' Director, Larry was the one responsible for Gorgas's films with John. Once he met John and viewed his work, he knew that John could capture the natural world he envisioned.

"I manage the Gorgas Science Foundation's nature reserve at El Cielo, Mexico. When I first met John, he suggested we make a film there.

"He started us down the road in doing films and showed us a new way to look at nature, and the things that God presents to us out in the forest.

"We worked together on four films and I found him a pleasure to work with. He was a humble man who always made sure other people were recognized.

"We traveled into the high altitudes, in the rain forest with its high humidity and abundant insect life. We experienced temperature extremes – the heat and the cold. John never complained.

"He would set up a blind, spend eight-to-ten hours waiting to shoot ten seconds of good footage.

"I'm most impressed with the things John left with us – the body of work, the way he tried to bring nature and the beauty of birds to others. He changed many of us.

"He mentored the young people we have working with us today."

Sandesh Kadur

Sandesh is a native of India who received his education at the University of Texas Brownsville. He met John while working with the Gorgas Science Foundation. His documentaries are shown on National Geographic, BBC, Discovery and Animal Plant. He is currently in India working on another project.

Sandesh shared the following memories: I remember glimpses of John at the screening for *El Cielo – Forest in the Clouds*, long before I ever met him. John was in a smart tuxedo (or maybe a smart suit). At the end of the screening he got up to a huge round of applause and charmed the audience with his talk. John Bax was a hero and all of the students were too scared to get too close. I mean, what does one say, what does one talk about with him, what does one ask… too many questions, so best to admire from a distance. First of all, we didn't call him John – it was Mr. Bax.

I can't quite remember who introduced me to John um, Mr. Bax, but I'm pretty sure it was Mr. Norman Richard – my long time mentor and professor with whom I shared a passion in natural history. In our very first meeting he set me straight. I addressed him as Mr. Bax, to which he immediately said, "Call me John…" Of course that took a while for me to get comfortable enough to say John, but he corrected me each time I said Mr. Bax, so very quickly I changed to addressing him as he is so fondly called by all - John.

Watching his documentaries were a source of pure inspiration. His skill, talent and patience were obvious in everything he captured. I wished that I had come to the US sooner, so perhaps I may have had an opportunity to assist John in the making of those wonderful documentaries. Nevertheless, Mr. (Larry) Lof came up with an idea to make a documentary on the mountain range near where I was from in southern India. He asked if John would be interested, he asked if I'd be happy to take John to India and assist him in the field and put together a documentary on the Western Ghats. I was overjoyed. I couldn't believe that an opportunity had come up wherein I would get to spend six months being an apprentice to John Bax!!

Summer fast approached and I began making contacts and getting things ready for the journey back to India. A few days before the trip, John called me over the phone. He was very silent on the other end, until he finally spoke, "Sandesh, I don't think I can go on this trip."

I was stunned into silence for a moment, until I mustered up courage to ask why?

He simply said, "I don't know, I think I'm getting too old." I knew he didn't want to say that.

This was way back in 1997. John continued to film all the way until 2011. His mind was still active and willing, but his body needed to rest.

Seth Patterson and Sandesh Kadur

During the time after 1997, John and I became much closer. He admired the production of *Sahyadris – Mountains of the Monsoon* and wholeheartedly supported my efforts. To me it was a great moment when John shook my hand at the end of the screening and wished me well. He knew what it takes to be behind the camera. Now when we shook hands it was something like a brotherhood, a camaraderie, wherein he welcomed me with the words, "You made it!"

Maybe John not coming to India was a test. A test to see if I could persevere till the end or give up mid-way and accept defeat. Perseverance, patience, and passion are the driving forces behind a filmmaker and no doubt, John had all these attributes in ample quantity. I still wish I could have spent time with John in the field. Not only is he an excellent filmmaker, but also an excellent naturalist. His field skills and ability to track down nesting birds or attract hummingbirds into his caravan was amazing.

Another really cool thing about John was that he was so quick to adapt to change. When the world moved away from film and into digital, John was at first apprehensive, but he quickly realized the quality and the cost-savings in this new format allowed him to shoot freely for hours and hours without worrying about developing costs etc. which would've been a problem with his traditional film.

Furthermore he took things a step further by leaping into digital editing on a laptop. While I don't think he bothered about learning how to email, he certainly took up the complicated task of editing clips of his videos and continued making short films of life in south Texas. Over time John amassed a wealth of footage. Till the end he never gave up.

He strove to share the natural world with those around him. His joy and enthusiasm at sharing his videos was one of the most admirable traits about him. I'll miss our long conversations of stories behind the scenes that only John with his lovely Belgian accent could narrate. I hope his films continue to live on and inspire a new generation to care about the planet we live on.

Seth Patterson

Seth is a nature photographer who has worked with the Gorgas Science Foundation since 2001. When he and John first met, John still spent most of his time filming. He sent the footage to Gorgas where Seth played a major role in the editing process. Later John edited his own video.

Seth chuckled when I asked him to share some of his adventures with John. I found out that they were total opposites. Seth works on a whim and takes off filming at a moment's notice. John was always prepared with his equipment, clothing, drinks, and food.

"John taught me so much. It was an honor to work with him," Seth said.

"He was one of the first who took me under his wing and taught me to document birds and their habitat in a non-intrusive manner."

Seth shared a favorite story about John. A few years ago, Richard Moore, a television personality and photographer in Harlingen, joined the two of them on an outing to Laguna Atascosa National Wildlife Refuge to film a mother alligator with her young. When they arrived at the pond, "Mom" was caring for approximately thirty babies. The babies crawled all over their mother or swam close by her side. Richard, John and Seth set up their equipment on an eight-foot embankment and each captured the scene. Richard and Seth began haranguing each other about climbing down the embankment to get a head-on shot of the mother.

"You go, I'm not going down in that mud," and similar comments became the game of the day. While they were enjoying the banter, John suddenly crawled down the embankment with his camera in hand. There he was – shooting eye-level film of the alligator family and the two much-younger guys were still sitting on the bank.

Seth laughed when he told the story of an eighty-year-old John in the forefront as usual. Seth went back to the pond the next day. The mother alligator was about fourteen feet away. A patch of sunlight lit the pond about halfway between Seth and the alligator. He wanted that alligator in the sunlight so he sat down and wiggled his fingers in the water. In a flash, the alligator dove in the water and headed toward him. Seth admitted that he moved fast that day.

When Seth was working on his recent book, *El Valle*, John helped him find some of the best locations. They shared locations if they found something to shoot or film. One day Seth headed down the Old Military Highway (US 281) into Brownsville. He spotted some anhingas and cormorants in a resaca and called John.

They borrowed a canoe from John's friend, Wally, to try for some close-up shots. They hoped for shallow water where they could get out of the canoe and film. John, prepared as usual, had his equipment ready and wore his waders. They had to get down a steep muddy embankment to get the canoe in the water. Seth suggested that they leave the equipment in the truck until they had the canoe in the water.

As they stepped into the canoe, it flipped. When Seth came up, he couldn't see any sign of John. He was worried about the weight of John's waders once they filled with water, or maybe he was stuck in the mud. When John surfaced, he saw the problems that concerned John. The water was chest high, the bottom was muddy, John's waders were full of water, and the two of them had to wrestle the canoe back to shore and up the embankment.

Seth shared his amazement at John's computer accomplishments. "When I first introduced John to a computer, he didn't even know what the mouse was or how it worked. He worked with focused attention to attain the skill where he could edit his own HD video. It's another example of his incredible patience and persistence."

Scarlet Colley is a Port Isabel dolphinologist, director of the Sea Life Center, birder and Seth's mother. "Mom had heard there was a Mangrove Warbler and she wanted to find a nest and document it as the first sighting in the United States. She called John to locate the bird nest and he went with her to the site and sure enough, John found the nest.

Madeleine Sandefur

Madeleine is an avid birder, photographer and traveler. She lives in Laguna Vista, Texas, and formed a friendship with John and Alice.

"I met this kind, unassuming man and his wife on the boardwalk at South Padre Island. I had no idea who they were, but they were busy setting up some video equipment, and later she was helping him film some action there."

Somewhat later, Madeleine put two and two together, and was embarrassed that she had not immediately recognized them. "I quickly learned more about his life's passion and work with birds, and feel lucky to have collected several of his videos, from some early ones shot in Mexico to some of his latest ones, filmed right in our backyard, so to speak.

"In time, I was fortunate to become better acquainted with John and Alice. They were always very generous with their time, giving presentations to various groups and sharing their knowledge.

"John instinctively knew where and how to find those nests, but with him, it was ALWAYS about the birds; they came first! I'll never forget: when he gave a presentation to our club at the SPI Birding Center, he mentioned a nest of Least Bitterns he had discovered. After the presentation, I asked him if he'd share the location with us.

A frown immediately crept onto his face; he was VERY reluctant to do that because he didn't want "people to disturb them".... We will never forget John; he will be missed by many!"

Steve Sinclair

Steve has a forty-plus-year history in the newspaper industry and is a seasoned photographer. He met John about twelve years ago on the boardwalk on South Padre Island.

"I found a coachwhip snake and saw that John had his equipment set up. I didn't realize he was looking for birds. I walked over to him and asked him if he'd like to film the snake. After he finished, he wanted me to look at a bird he'd seen. That was the beginning."

Steve marveled at John's incredible sense of direction and distance as well as his ability to instantly size up a place and know what birds might be there. "He knew all the roads like the back of his hand."

Steve offered two good stories about John. "I lost a bet with him once." He was at John's house where they had been observing migratory hummingbirds. Steve had taken a number of photos of a particular bird and told John he wished he could take them inside.

'If you want me to, I can bring them into the kitchen," John offered.

"I laughed and bet him that he couldn't do it. I should have known better," Steve said. "John grabbed the feeder, stood still, talked to the bird and slowly moved the feeder a little closer to the house. He kept doing so until he had the birds in the kitchen.

"As usual, John told me I could do that too if I wanted to. He didn't realize the gift he had."

One spring, John and Steve were taking pictures in the vacant lot next to John's house. Steve hoped to photograph some quail. When John finished, Steve asked him, "How will I get the quail to come?"

"I'll call them for you," John said. Much to Steve's amazement, John walked into his house, looked out the bathroom window and whistled. The quail came and Steve took photos.

"We had a lot of fun looking for Barn Owls. We found their nests and we divided the days of the week for filming. Seth and I each took a day a week. John was free to go the other days." Steve captured a beautiful shot of the five baby owls..

John took Steve in to show him the setup of the owls. Steve noticed some cars going by with poachers. John told him "I got away from the Nazis. Do you think I'm going to worry about a few poachers?" Steve later wrote about this for an article in the *Coastal Current.*

"John told us about a palm tree on the campus of the University of Texas-Brownsville that was home to parrots, Green Parakeets, Eastern Screech

Owls, Black-bellied Whistling Ducks, Golden-fronted Woodpeckers, and Muscovy Ducks. Green Herons and Night Herons were near the tree. Seth and I couldn't believe that they all nested in the same tree, but John was right. We found them."

Tom Vezo

Tom's work appears in publications such as *Audubon*, *Bird Watcher's Digest*, *Birder's World*, *National Geographic*, *National Wildlife Federation*, *Nature Conservancy*, *Outdoor Photographer*, *Sierra*, and *WildBird*.

He worked with John and Tony Mercieca for several years in Texas and Canada. In his book, *Wings of Spring: Courtship, Nesting, and Fledging*, he wrote:

"My newfound friends who helped me get some photos for this book, John and Alice Bax and Tony Mercieca. John is a wildlife filmmaker whose work I'd admired for years before I met him. He's made more than twenty films for the Discovery Channel and *Profiles of Nature*. I've never photographed with anyone who works harder in the field than John. He possesses an incredible intellect and instinct of the natural world that is extraordinary. I would also like to thank his wife, Alice, who has kept us well fed on the road in Texas and Canada with her wonderful cooking.

Tony Mercieca has been photographing for more than thirty-five years and has been instrumental in improving stop-action flash photography. He builds his own high speed flash units and was probably the first photographer to create and use the Fresnel flash extension. I've had the pleasure of working with these two guys for the past three years and have gained a tremendous amount of knowledge from them."

Lee Zieger

Lee is a long-time Rio Grande Valley resident, a business man, conservationist, and photographer. He owns an RV park in Brownsville and he met John in the mid 1980s when John was showing his films throughout the Valley. John booked several shows each winter at Lee's park. After his work with the Gorgas Science Foundation, John sold his tapes and showed his work on film and later moved to digital video and DVDs.

"I would book John for several shows a winter." Lee said. "On the nights we showed a film, John always entered the park in his pickup with a canoe on top. Everyone knew who was coming. It was great advertising for his show. Having new shows was important to keep the interest up. At that time John had more than twelve shows he could present. He was having his film professionally edited and a voice dubbed in.

"On some of his last video with the easier do it yourself equipment, he and Alice did the narrations. John kept busy each winter entertaining and teaching the Rio Grande Valley Winter Texans about wildlife from South America to Northern Canada. The Winter Texans would buy his tapes and take them home back north for their family and friends to enjoy spreading the word.

Alice remembers that years later in Arizona, she and John met a woman who knew him through a tape she had received as a gift.

"John spent his summers making new films all over the American Continents. He completed his last DVD, *The Treasures of Deep South Texas – 2*, in 2011."

In the late fall and early spring, John and Lee explored potential photography locations. They scoured Brownsville and San Benito looking for parrots and other birds. Since Laguna Atascosa National Wildlife Refuge and a neighboring ranch were among John's favorite places, they searched the back roads and their regular "hot spots." John usually found photo opportunities without interfering with natural wildlife patterns.

"Until the last, John was eager to ride around visiting his favorite bird photography hot spots and looking for new ones," Lee said. "John really enjoyed the bird cavity dwellers most, like the parrots, woodpeckers, titmouse, owls and, believe it or not, the Black-bellied Whistling Ducks. The parrot captured his imagination with its brilliant colors, squawking voice, public interest and activity around the cavity nest. Watching and listening to them was fun.

"John's fascination with hummingbirds and raptors came to life in his videos. He was great at getting hummingbirds to land on his hand and fingers. His back yard bird display brought in many local bird species like Bobwhite Quail, Long-billed and Curve-billed Thrashers, Orange-headed Warblers, Northern Cardinals, Olive Sparrows, plus a Harris's Hawk would drop in when hungry. Many of these birds do not go much further north in Texas much less the USA, which made them really special. It was always fun and interesting to be around John."

Lee found new locations, photography methods and new approaches from their expeditions. John knew how to find the birds and the locations for the best shots.

"He was always able and willing to knock around ideas that would lead to new and different approaches to the best possible picture or video," Lee said.

Lee shared the following story about John's backyard explorations.

"Watching John feeding the wild creatures in his back yard amazed me. He and Alice fed them most mornings and afternoons. Alice would hand the food over a fence to John. He put water out and peanut butter on dead logs first – cleaning the water pan when necessary. The birds, especially quail, at this point seemed to know it was their turn with John and Alice's seed mix. It was like a farmer feeding his chickens. John whistled while he put out the food and the quails, sparrows, and others would start coming out. He then sat down, sometimes with his camera and other times just to watch, while the birds enjoyed a good meal."

Chapter 10: More Lives than a Cat

"Luck followed John all his life." Alice Bax

Alice believes good fortune smiled on John throughout his life. Even though he grew up in a harsh era, spent much of his youth dodging the Nazis and had limited education, he flourished. He possessed an incredible ability to focus on his goals but maybe he charmed fate along the way. Alice created a list of sixteen times she believes that John "dodged the bullet." They are mentioned throughout this book. Two are mentioned below.

His strong will, good health, and determination helped him to walk out of the Tundra at age fifty, after filming there in the spring, earning him the respect and admiration of a much younger man, Larry Patterson.

One fall while fishing alone on a favorite secluded lake, his canoe tipped over. John thought he would drown. His heavy boots, winter jacket and two anchors made it almost impossible to move. His determination got him to the opposite shore. Pure luck kept him from suffering from hypothermia because he had to right the canoe and gather everything into it, paddle back across the lake, walk a half mile or so to the car, and drive back to our trailer.

Leo (John's brother) and Alice agreed that John was always lucky. He never suffered from a snake bite nor had an encounter with a ferocious animal.

"John always believed that anyone could do what he did. He'd tell me it just takes patience. I don't think he was aware of his natural affinity for nature and his special gifts," Alice said.

From time to time, John suffered severe sunburn. Two of the worst cases: in Ecuador on his lips and in Bonaire on his feet.

When John and Alice camped, they slept in the truck. Once during the night, Alice heard something thrashing around. They had been to the store and left the groceries on the table.

They got up to find a bear rummaging for food. They both started banging on pans to frighten him away, but the bear didn't leave. He ate all their food.

"We fed the bear," Alice said.

Early in the morning, John got up to clean up the mess.

"I met the bear on the road and he gave me a list of groceries he'd like to have," he joked when he finished.

Sure enough, the bear came back the next morning. The campground manager had set some meat in a cage and captured him.

John never wanted to tell the people in authority what had happened because he always thought he'd done something wrong.

"He never wanted to take the chance that people wouldn't let him continue with his crazy business," Alice said.

One of the first trips in Laguna Atascosa National Wildlife Refuge, his truck got stuck. He had to walk out of the refuge and home to Rio Hondo. The next day, he had to go back and get his truck.

John Bax, Teacher and Mentor

"John's unique voice captivated his audiences." Lee Zieger, businessman and photographer

Many friends, acquaintances, photographers and birders sought John's advice. He mentored students, especially Seth Patterson and Sandesh Kadur. Groups from Belgium and Canada came to the Valley to bird with him. Dr. George Peck visited several times.

Two Belgians visited John in Canada to make a film. One had already visited him in south Texas. Together they traipsed all over Manitoba and found the footage they wanted. At the end of the film, John and one of the guys are dancing to radio music.

Two young men who visited John in Texas wanted to add to their life list. In addition to the birds, they loved the large portions that local restaurants served.

Mostly people came in hopes of finding birds they hadn't seen. A friend made a film after his visit. Mieke Leppens and her family, from Belgium, came to bird in Texas. John became a mentor to her son, Hakan, and taught him about birds and birding. They developed a close relationship that lasted until John's death.

"They were all grateful to use John's talent in finding birds and they all acknowledged that they never would have seen nearly as many birds on their own," Alice said

"John's unique voice captivated his audiences," Lee Zieger said. "His European heritage gave him a sometimes hard-to-understand yet very interesting brogue that kept his audience on the edge of their seats anxiously awaiting his next word."

The man who in his youth became ill at the thought of speaking in class turned into a man completely at ease when talking about his favorite subject.

John made presentations in RV parks throughout the Valley in the 1980s and 1990s. After he began filming for the Gorgas Science Foundation in the 1990s, he increased his speaking engagements and expanded into birding festivals. He traveled up and down the Rio Grande Valley. In 1998, he was the featured presenter at the Imperial Beach Bird Fest in California. He attended and spoke at festivals whenever asked. John enjoyed the Gorgas Science Foundation's film premieres because he had the opportunity to talk about his experiences and to watch people's reactions to his work.

John visited birding and nature centers, festivals, RV parks and campgrounds. He discussed his films and birding. He made nearly 200 presentations over the next few years and personally sold more than 2,000 copies of his last four films.

He loved educating people and answering their questions about the birds. His natural charm endeared him to audiences. South Texas was a perfect place for him to connect with birders and photographers.

Nine World Birding Centers offer unique bird habitat up and down the Rio Grande Valley. John loved to visit them and share his stories with fellow birders. He was a frequent visitor to Laguna Atascosa National Wildlife Refuge and other nature preserves throughout the region.

John continued speaking before groups and showing his films almost until the end of his life. When his aneurysm began leaking, pain engulfed him and he could no longer get out to film or talk about his birds, he knew the end was near.

A Hiking Weekend with his Grandfather

When Jeff Bax was eleven or twelve, John, his grandfather asked him to go on a hiking weekend through Fanshawe Park (Fanshawe Conservation Area in London, Ontario). Eager to camp and spend time with his grandfather, Jeff looked forward to the trip. When he had camped with his parents, they had their own tents, sleeping bags, food cooked on a camp stove, clean washrooms and showers.

John and Jeff left from John's trailer carrying their backpacks, camera equipment and food. They hiked the remote trails and saw no one the entire weekend. They climbed over boulders as well as up and down a few cliffs. They walked through streams and gullies. John pointed out wildlife, especially birds. At certain spots, they stopped and hid in the bushes. John waited until he had good wildlife filming opportunities.

When evening came, they stopped, cooked dinner over an open fire and set up camp for the night. They slept on a large flat rock with just a blanket over them. Jeff heard strange sounds throughout the night. John always explained what it was and Jeff wasn't afraid.

"Jeff came home with a greater appreciation of what his grandfather did for a living," his mother, Maureen Bax, said. "He saw his love for his work and realized it wasn't his grandfather's job, it was his lifestyle."

Jeff grew up to appreciate nature and photography. He enjoys hiking and searching for astrophotography opportunities. He is a long-distance walker like John. Jeff recently received his PhD in medicine (cancer research).

Andre, Mieke and Hakan Leppens, Belgium

The Leppens family became friends with John and Alice during their 1993 visit to Turnhout. John went to Belgium to show his film, *At a Bend in a Mexican River*. The following day, Mieke and Hakan Leppens joined John in a nature walk in the Liereman. Afterwards, Hakan wrote the following letter.

> Dear John Bax
>
> I am Hakan Leppens. I am 10 years. And would like to correspond with you. I counted birds on 28.02.1993. The result was.
>
> Great Tit- 34, Blue Tit- 10, Long-tailed Tit- 5, Robin- 3, Wood pigeons- 2, Willow Tit- 2, Marsh Tit- 1, Blackbirds- 2, Dunnock 1, Crested Tit- 1
>
> These birds at the feeder, I counted in our garden. The blue heron is regularly catching fish in our pond. The kingfisher takes post on the branch that hangs over the pond. When the sun shines, he has beautiful colors. We have observed him as he caught a fish. The squirrels are even awake. They jump from one tree to another tree. They love the sunflower seeds and peanuts… As you can see I am a true friend of nature… With this I end my letter.

Greetings to you and Alice
(translated through Google translation)

onze intrek in ons nieuwe huis was formidabel.

De ontmoetig met John Bax.

John Bax kwam in 1993 naar Turnhout.
Hij is een bekend natuurfilmer.
Ik vroeg om met hem te corresponderen.
Met Kerstmis stuurde hij een kaart.
In juli schreef ik een brief terug naar John.

Een paar weken later kreeg ik een brief terug.
John heeft al veel films gemaakt over colibri's   kolibries
Dat zijn zeer kleine vogeltjes van snavel tot staart
zijn ze 4cm groot.
Zijn laatste film heet: The treasures of the Rio Grandedelta.
Deze film werd gemaakt in Brazilië.

Dit is mijn leven.

School report that Hakan wrote about the nature trip.

John regularly corresponded with Hakan and his parents until his death. The Leppens visited John and Alice in Texas. Meike wrote about their trip:

> Travelogue 1998.
>
> Finally happened April 4, 1998. We left our friend, nature filmmaker John Bax, in Texas. Since 1993, we corresponded with him about the nature experiences in the Kempen.
>
> John and Alice stood waiting for us (at the Harlingen airport) … The next morning after breakfast we drove to Laguna Atascosa National Wildlife Refuge. The Mexican squirrel greeted us. The Least Grebe, the Great Blue Heron, the Great Egret and the Snow Egret. Suddenly I said to John, "Which bird is that?" as a cormorant on the water and so many more waterfowl passed in review. Alligators sometimes up to 6 feet long were impressive.
>
> On Monday we visited Santa Ana Refuge. The hanging moss in the trees was impressive! Alice said in the morning that we would see many birds. John joked: "If you spot a bird, which I've never seen, you get a diamond ring. As far as we now know, John has never had to give a ring. The most rare sighting that day was the Fulvous Whistling Duck.
>
> South Padre Island… John wanted to show us the rails. Very quietly we went over the wooden walkway, which was among the reeds. John clapped his hands in order to lure the rails.
>
> Thursday John led us to Rio Colorado Arroyo. John, Andre and Hakan fished, using shrimp as bait. Alice and I took root on the waterfront, each with a book at hand. The sun was hot that day. Hakan's ears were seriously burned.
>
> Friday John and Alice took us to Bentsen State Park. The call of the Chachalaca was very special and remained in our heads for days. The splendor of the Indigo Bunting, Altamira Oriole and the Red Cardinal was remarkable. During lunch we talked a bit with John and he told the story of his hat. "The Tilley hat will not blow off your head, not even at a wind speed of 100 kilometers per hour. There is also built in ventilation, and you get lifetime warranty. If something is wrong, send it in and you get a new one…
>
> John, thank you for the ornithological field knowledge that you

taught us and for the years that we shared friendship. You will forever have a place in our hearts.

Mieke – Andre - Hakan

Hakan and John – South Padre Island

L-R: Alice, John, Hakan, Mieke, Andre

John's Letters

Although John was not a prolific letter writer, his papers included copies of a few of the letters he wrote to producers and friends over the years.

In 1980, John wrote a query letter to Manitou Productions in Ontario. In it, he references his early filming days.

> *Being the adventurous type, I immigrated to Canada in 1965. Excited by the Canadian wildlife, I decided to capture it on film. In 1966, I invested some money in an 8mm camera and set out on my filming expedition. Most of my knowledge of cameras came from reading materials. With some firsthand experience and motivation from a few professional people, I finally graduated to a 16mm camera in 1969...*

John frequently wrote letters to Bob Bocking, his editor, detailing filming incidents. In Jamaica, he noted,

> *I filmed Mrs. Salmon sitting on her porch while many species of Hummers visited the Hummingbird feeder she had in her hand.*

In another letter to Bob, he wrote,

> *In Jamaica I filmed the Western Streamertail and Jamaican Mango,*

young ones in the nest. Also the female Cuban Emerald feeding two young ones in the nest.

In 1981, he wrote to Bob about his Honduras trip:

Things did not go as I planned in Honduras. I got stuck because of a bridge that collapsed. After 10 days waiting I learned that there was no money available to repair the bridge and since this was the only road to get through I had to come back, so after a little more than one month and 6,000 miles I arrived here in Arizona close to the Mexican border...

On my way back from Honduras, in Guatemala in the middle of the night they were shooting all around me so I ran out of the trailer into a corn-field where I stayed for 3-4 hours. I saw many trucks passing with soldiers and I think they were shooting at them. Things are not good in Central America. The little towns are dirty and almost impassable at times. Also the people are very poor and not friendly towards the Gringos.

In 1998, he wrote a note to Dr. Fernando Ortiz,

Hi Fernando, We are with our friends, Tony and Peg Mercieca in San Diego, and learned about the Sun Angel nest with 3 eggs in it, from your note on the net... I am working on another Hummingbird film; hopefully it will be finished in 1998. In 1997 we went to Jamaica and Cuba, finally....

He kept in touch with his many international friends through letters and Christmas cards. He loved sending and receiving correspondence. In his letters, he kept his friends and colleagues up to date on his filming and birding experiences. In his letters back home to Belgium, he easily mixed Dutch and English.

John and his brother, Leo, remained in communication and visited each other until Leo's death. Leo appeared in the film, *The Man Who Loved Birds*.

John's Life List

By 1988, John listed a total of 309 species with nests and 658 birds in his life list (shown in Appendix III). It is incomplete because John saw many new species in his Central and South American trips. It is updated as much as possible from individual trips and films. With his many trips to Central and South America, the list would certainly include hundreds of new bird sightings and filmings.

As the excerpted notes throughout the book indicate, John recorded every detail of his trips, from species verified and recorded to daily expenses and health issues.

His journals give a glimpse into his dedication and the years he spent following and recording birds and their habits.

It's little wonder that photographers and birders continued to ask John to help them find the birds.

Book Three: Films

Introduction

"I've never done still photography. I always wanted to do movies. I prefer to shoot living action.

"Video cameras don't have a variable speed and can't take slow-motion shots. Most professional nature filmmakers use cameras that take 16mm film; it produces the best quality for TV master films.

"Sometimes I photograph from a blind. I use three lenses, a close up, a 12 to 120mm zoom and a telephoto that magnifies nine times. That's equal to a 450mm lens on a still camera.

"My first film was a nature film entitled 'Nesting Time.' It was my first effort and many professional film makers who saw it encouraged me to go professional."

John Bax

Many of John's films are not available for today's technology. He filmed first with Super 8mm and then a Bolex 16mm movie camera.

His later work for the Gorgas Science Foundation was released in VHS but most of it is out of production. When he got his digital camera, he began producing his own DVDs. They are currently available.

The titles discussed in the following chapters were the ones accessible to the author.

Birds of the Arctic Tundra, 1984

3. BIRDS OF THE ARCTIC TUNDRA

John Bax is an experienced and dedicated wildlife cinematographer who devoted three summers to a film study of the wildfowl species that summer in the Canadian Arctic. Featured in this program are the behavioural patterns of the snow geese, whose giant flocks fill the sky on their annual migration to these remote nesting sites. Many other species are recorded here including the red necked loon and rare footage of the Arctic loon.

Profiles of Nature documentary

This project took John to Alaska, the Yukon, Hudson Bay and Baffin Island. Joining a group of students and researchers from the University of Western Ontario, John traveled to the mouth of the McConnell River and the McConnell River Bird Sanctuary to film the nesting habits of snow geese.

Covered in Chapter 1 of Book Two, this trip produced film that was used in a *Profiles of Nature* documentary by Ellis Vision Production in association with CFCN TV, from 1984 – 2001. John served as an advisor.

Some of the species covered in the film include:

Arctic Grouse (Alaska Ptarmigan)
Arctic Loon
Arctic Tern
Eider Duck
Lesser Snow Goose or Blue Goose
Parasitic Jaeger
Red-throated Loon
Sandhill Crane
Semi-palmated Plover
Snow Bunting
Snow Goose
Willow Ptarmigan

The Man Who Loved Birds, 1986

"Traveling the world and taking pictures of every bird known to man – that's my dream." The Man Who Loved Birds

Produced by KEG Productions, this film was the first to recount John's life.

The film begins with John getting up close and personal with the birds — feeding a hummingbird from a spoon, petting and feeding berries to Cedar Waxwing babies and petting a Killdeer.

Recognizing John's extraordinary talent, the film covers John's filming career from the early days in Canada with footage of the Snow Geese, Western Grebes, and White Pelicans. John's burgeoning interest in hummingbirds takes center stage as John begins to travel south.

From his first trip to Texas to his trips to Central and South America, John captures new and rare birds in their natural habitats.

Incredible footage of "water walking" Western Grebes, baby American Bitterns, and the Andean Hillstar Hummingbird shows the hours required for John to capture the birds on film. The film ends with John looking forward to his next adventure.

The Man Who Loved Birds was sold to Belgium TV and the city of Turnhout watched it en masse.

Species covered in the film include:

Alligators
American Bittern
American Goldfinch
Andean Hillstar Hummingbird
Arctic Loon
Arctic Tern
Black-backed Woodpecker
Three-toed Woodpecker
Black-tailed Trainbearer
Brown Thrasher
Cedar Waxwing
Eared Grebe
Evening Grosbeak
Giant Hummingbird
Gray Jay
Great Gray Owl
Green Violetear
Killdeer
King Eider
Least Bittern
Long-billed Starthroat Hummingbird
Magnolia Warbler
Northern Oriole
Parasitic Jaeger
Pileated Woodpecker
Prairie Warbler
Red-breasted Merganser
Red-headed Woodpecker
Red-necked Grebe
Red-throated Loon
Sandhill Crane

Snow Goose
Sparkling Violetear
Sword-billed Hummingbird
Western Grebe
White Pelican
Yellow-throated Warbler

The Treasure of Madera Canyon: John Bax in Arizona, 1989

This film featured John's expedition in Madera Canyon and was produced by KEG Productions in 1989. Bob Bocking continued to edit John's films.

John hiked the desert floor, grasslands, dry riverbeds and all over the seven highest peaks of the Santa Rita Mountains in search of nesting birds. He found many species of birds including the Phainopepla (a member of the Silky Flycatcher family) and the Elegant Trogon (only about a dozen pairs live in the US).

"It is a unique place…people think it's desert but it isn't… "I worked without the mosquitoes which is very important." John's beginning commentary set the tone for the film.

John, at sixty-four years of age, explored new horizons and filmed many species of nesting birds. He hiked with his backpack eight hours a day looking for, and filming, birds. When he found birds, he went back to camp and returned with his tripod and camera.

He set up hummingbird feeders around his trailer where he began each day by observing the feeding birds. He continually moved the feeders closer to the trailer and patiently waited with his two cameras ready to film. He filmed at 50 frames a second to slow down the hummingbirds' wings.

He began to experiment. He moved a feeder inside his trailer and over the next days, filmed multiple species of hummingbirds as they came inside to feed.

He found a Costa's Hummingbird nest and filmed himself feeding sugar water to a female while she incubated her eggs. Another time, he stood holding a feeder for half an hour. The birds flew around his hand; one perched on his finger. He conducted another experiment, putting a feeder in his mouth. A hummingbird drank from the feeder.

"Once I see a bird, I have a feeling…if the bird will accept me or not... I let that bird do his thing…then I come up with these crazy ideas…to have them perch on my finger…".

John placed his camera within inches of the feeders as he sat a little distance away with the remote control.

He had traveled all over America in search of hummingbirds and Madera Canyon lived up to his dreams. He filmed the Broad-billed Hummingbird, one of his favorites. Hummingbirds he filmed: Magnificent, Black-chinned, Rufous, Broad-tailed, Calliope, Costa's and Anna's.

In addition to the Phainopepla and the Elegant Trogon, he filmed many species: Acorn Woodpecker, Cooper's Hawk, Ash-throated Flycatcher, Brown-crested Flycatcher, Dusky-capped Flycatcher, Blue Grosbeak, Western Tanager, Mourning Dove, White-crowned Sparrow, Lucy's Warbler, Black-headed Grosbeak, Northern Oriole, Gambel's Quail, Lazuli Bunting, House Finch, Yellow-breasted Chat, Wilson's Warbler, Scott's Oriole and the Elf Owl.

He discovered and educated people about the mating and nesting habits of different species. He talked about the problems - poisonous snakes and scorpions. "I am careful. I respect nature," he told his audience.

John took his time setting up each shot; sometimes it took an hour. He worked from a blind. He adjusted his camera speed. To shoot the Elf Owl, he filmed at 10 – 18 frames a second and ran it at 24.

When he found a Vermillion Flycatcher nest, he spent days at the nest waiting for the right moment. He observed that both parents caught insects and fed their young. The chicks were ten days old. He found a nesting Lucy's Warbler in a rotting tree cavity. These birds are found only in the Southwest. He filmed a Cactus Wren living in a cholla cactus and Scott's Orioles in yuccas. He captured a short-horned lizard eating his way through a colony of ants.

"I like working by myself…this is my whole life…filming birds," John told his audience.

Journey to Brazoria, 1990

"John Bax is no stranger to this region…to the refuges of south Texas." From Journey to Brazoria

"It's early spring…and London, Ontario's John Bax is on another exciting adventure…a one-man bird safari to a lonely refuge on the windblown Gulf Coast of Texas…where alligators raise their young in marshes filled with colorful nesting birds…where 270 bird species have been sighted…a haunting coastal landscape with a poetic, almost magical name…Brazoria." Thus began the film, *Journey to Brazoria.*

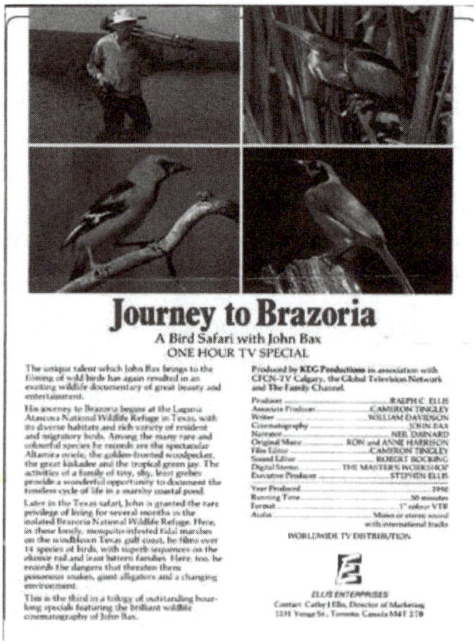

The film begins at Laguna Atascosa NWR with White Pelicans. John tells the audience that it has been one of his favorite places for the last six years, "Marvelous for bird watchers to see all the bird species."

John originally came to Laguna Atascosa in search of the Least Grebe, the smallest of all the North American grebes. "Laguna Atascosa Refuge is just one of my favorite places… I love it."

In the film, he showed pairs of Least Grebes constructing floating nest platforms of decaying aquatic vegetation. He observed that the sexes look alike and mating takes place on the floating nest.

He found that during their twenty-three-day incubation, the male provided food for the female. Once the first chick appears, it can take up to four days for the rest of the eggs to hatch. The mother carries the eggshells away from the nest to distract predators while she is away. The film shows the young chicks learning to swim and riding around on their parents' backs.

The Least Grebes are good swimmers and divers. They spend a lot of time preening to keep their feathers in good condition. John caught all of this action on film.

John filmed alligators raising their young. He found the tree-hanging nests of the Altamira Oriole, a species found in no other region of the United States or Canada. He filmed all three species of kingfishers — Green, Ringed and Belted — that are found in the Lower Rio Grande Valley.

John's biggest surprise in Laguna Atascosa was finding and filming nesting Black-chinned Hummingbirds here. He captured the mother feeding her newly hatched babies. He considered it a rare find as the refuge is at their extreme eastern range limit.

John captured great footage of the green anole, the only species of anoles (of the reptile family) that is native to North America.

Birds filmed (most nesting) in Laguna Atascosa:

Altamira Oriole
Belted Kingfisher
Black-bellied Whistling Duck
Black-chinned Hummingbird
Brown-crested Flycatcher
Eastern Screech Owl
Golden-fronted Woodpecker
Great Egret
Great Kiskadee
Great-tailed Grackle
Green Jay
Green Kingfisher
Inca Dove
Northern Mockingbird
Plain Chachalaca
Red-winged Blackbird
Ringed Kingfisher
White-tailed Kite

The second part of the film takes place in Brazoria National Wildlife Refuge. Once he set up his trailer, he started each day at 6:30, searched for nests and filmed until dark.

Because the rails are secretive birds, he found it difficult to find their nests. The film shows him day after day in his canoe searching through the marshes. John found five nests, all close to the water. He worried that the birds would all drown and the eggs would be lost. When he returned, he found one bird drowned but the others had built up their nests to provide more security.

He found a King Rail nest and observed Clapper Rails often nest next to them. The sexes share the parenting duties. The female lays an egg a day for about twelve days.

John usually filmed from a blind about three yards away from the nest. He again used two cameras and the film shows multiple shots of him in his canoe, in the marsh or near a nest. Some birds allowed him to film them without a blind.

He encountered his share of difficulties, usually in the form of snakes and mosquitoes. He saw and filmed pit vipers, rattlers, cottonmouth and water moccasin as well as species that weren't harmful.

"Filming wildlife is hard. You have to be in shape," John said of his days trekking through the marshes. The biggest problem was the mosquitoes which he described as "not talking millions…billions and billions all the time."

John filmed alligators, armadillos, snakes, lizards, spotted gar, native plants, and wildflowers. "I am standing with this alligator (12 foot long) for four hours. I like it. I could take very good close-ups…plus the young ones which were crawling on the mother's head and back," he said.

He found fifteen nests of Least Bitterns — he filmed two. "Sometimes I think I'm crazy to do these things," he said.

Birds Filmed in Brazoria:

Black Vulture
Black-necked Stilt
Clapper Rail
Common Moorhen
Common Nighthawk
Eastern Kingbird
King Rail
Least Bittern
Purple Gallinule
Ruddy Turnstone
Turkey Vulture
Wilson's Plover

John's comment when asked why he endures the heat and mosquitoes: "I couldn't think of doing anything else. It was just the thing to do and I did it. I'm happy I did it."

At a Bend in the Mexican River, 1992

In 1992, the Gorgas Science Foundation in Brownsville, Texas, in conjunction with Texas Southmost College, produced *At a Bend in the Mexican River*, which featured John's work in northeastern Mexico.

Traveling to the end of a road, he arrived at a tropical river that ran through the region. Artist and ornithologist, George M. Sutton, first wrote about its natural beauty and scientific importance. John fell in love with its colors, sounds, and diversity. It was here that John found a buddy, a red-bellied squirrel that kept him company throughout his stay.

John discovered an unbelievable number of bird species, 255 within a few hours walk from the field station. In a land with only two seasons, wet and dry, John prepared to film them. He put out feeders and enjoyed the rewards of his efforts.

Altamira Orioles flocked to the oranges. So, unfortunately, did the Brown Jays, which John considered to be a scourge. Exciting species of hummingbirds ventured to John's feeders.

He filmed the Common Potoo, which is rare, that far north and has more than a three-foot wingspan. The Common Potoo sleeps in the daytime in an upright position. It looks like a dead stick.

John filmed butterflies, ants and the nesting habits of birds before the rains made his work impossible.

Larry Lof had asked Bob Bocking to work with John in Mexico.

"It was a wonderful collaboration resulting in some really good films," Bob said.

Some of the bird species in the film:

Amazon Kingfisher
Azure Crown

Barred Antshrike
Blue crowned Motmot
Boat-billed Flycatcher
Bronzed Cowbird
Brown Jay
Brown-crested Flycatcher
Buff-bellied Hummingbird
Bumblebee Hummingbird
Common Potoo
Ferruginous Pygmy Owl
Golden fronted Woodpecker
Gray-crowned Yellowthroat
Great Curassow
Green breasted Mango
Green Kingfisher
Groove-billed Ani
Hooded Oriole
Hummingbirds
Inca Dove
Lineated Woodpecker
Mountain Trogon
Olive Sparrow
Pale-billed Woodpecker
Red-headed Parrot
Ringed Kingfisher
Ruby-throated Hummingbird
Rufous Cap Brush Finch
Shy thicket Teamoo
Small blue-black Grosbeak
Wedge-tailed Sabrewing Hummingbird

El Cielo: Forest in the Clouds, 1993

The film focused on the mountain forest, Rancho del Cielo and its unique variety of northern and southern fauna in Tamaulipas, Mexico.

The film encompassed nearly every part of the 300,000-acre reserve placed under the United Nation's *Man and the Biosphere* program and documented the various species of endangered parrots and other birds that inhabit the forest.

The University of Texas and Texas Southmost College own a 60-acre mini-reserve in the middle of the larger reserve. The Gorgas Science Foundation often holds educational retreats there. Once again, Bob Bocking agreed to join the project.

John met with students and staff at Rancho del Cielo in a remote cloud forest that overlooks the river bend. UNESCO named El Cielo a biosphere preserve. Today it is protected by the Mexican government and is closed to the general public.

John found the reserve "one of the most beautiful and unique areas I've ever seen." He worked with the university over the next three years to finish the film.

"There were no modern conveniences and I had a lot of challenges. We had no vehicles and I walked miles every day. It was difficult but it was worth it. The only thing available was a mule."

The area's exquisite beauty and uniqueness struck John. "You're up in the clouds and it's completely different. I worked there for quite some time."

John's filming of El Cielo gave viewers a sense of the rain forest's beauty. With his two-camera filming, viewers watched him as he searched for birds and their nests. For four months, John hiked the mountainsides from dawn until dark in search of new species – particularly the Bumblebee Hummingbird. With the months of rain and the ever-present mist, his expeditions were soggy but successful.

"I recall camping high in the mountains of Mexico on a quest to film the Bumblebee Hummingbird," Bob Bocking recalled. "It is the world's smallest and was a challenge to film. I had never experienced pouring rain like we had on that trip. I was recording sound at the time and was able to capture the faint call of the tiny hummingbird.

"We filmed Macaws nesting in the canyon. Again I was lucky and captured their raucous calls."

Some of the birds shown in El Cielo film include:

Amazon Kingfisher
Barred Antshrike
Bronze-winged Woodpecker
Bumblebee Hummingbird
Common Potoo
Curassow
Hooded Grosbeak
Military Macaw
Motmot
Mountain Trogon
Ringed Kingfisher
Rufous-capped Brush Finch
White-eared Hummingbird

Treasures of the Rio Grande Delta, 1994

John had filmed in Texas since his first trip in 1988. When the Gorgas Science Foundation decided to produce a film on the Rio Grande Valley, John filmed several more years securing the footage.

The film covered the delta country from the Chihauhauan Desert in the west to the mouth of the Rio Grande River at the Gulf of Mexico.

He followed the river, filming its path and the natural world surrounding it. From the desert floor, wetlands, and the Gulf of Mexico, John documented the country's nature, habitat and history.

The delta of the Rio Grande is a special place. The species-rich natural community that is found along the river's banks flourishes in a transition zone in which the semi-arid tropics slowly give way to the temperate north. Several of the most endangered or threatened species live on the delta and can be found nowhere else in the U.S. or Mexico…

The delta has served as a crucible in which the history of North America was forged. The first battle of the Mexican War and the last battle of the Civil War were fought here. From the World Premiere of the film

The production team set an ambitious goal to show both the natural world and human history. Starting with shots of shorebirds and alligators, the film segued into early expeditions by the Spanish in the late 1500s to the important battles affecting both the US and Mexico. As late as the 1800s, palm trees and Spanish Moss-draped ebony trees covered much of the land. Civilization eventually cut off much of the water flow of the once-mighty river.

Tracing these changes in nature, agriculture, climate, and development, the film gave viewers a glimpse of the region's past glories. John's camera work focused on the delta's inhabitants from Red-crowned Parrots and horned toads to collared peccaries and ocelots.

In the film, John shared his enthusiasm for the region: "I recommend everybody to come here and see the wildlife and the Valley."

****

The film opened on November 3, 1994, to a crowd of more than 800 in Harlingen, Texas. At the 1995 Houston World Fest Film Festival, the film took 4th place, out of 4,000 entries.

Partial list of birds in the film:

Altamira Oriole
American Avocet
Belted Kingfisher
Black Skimmer
Black-bellied Whistling Duck
Black-crested Titmouse
Black-headed Oriole
Blue Grosbeak
Bobwhite Quail
Bronzed Cowbird
Buff-bellied Hummingbird
Common Nighthawk
Crested Caracara
Eastern Screech Owl
Great Kiskadee
Greater Roadrunner
Green Jay

Green Parakeet
Groove-billed Ani
Harris's Hawk
King Rail
Least Bittern
Least Grebe
Long-billed Thrasher
Mottled Duck
Northern Jacana
Painted Bunting
Plain Chachalaca
Purple Gallinule
Red-crowned Parrot
Ringed Kingfisher
Snowy Plover
Sora
Turkey Vulture
White Pelican
White-crowned Sparrow
Wild Turkey

A Passion for Birds, 1996

"John Bax is a humble man who has not really received his due. We hope that the next film will help to rectify this situation. In a year or so, you can join us for the premier of a film that honors an artist and a naturalist. It will be a film that does justice to John Bax and his film legacy." Gorgas Science Foundation

The above quote was from the Gorgas Science Foundation's announcement for *A Passion for Birds*. The film would showcase John's talent and the beauty of nature.

****

"For decades, John Bax searched the world to bring us his beautiful images of nature and, in particular, his special passion – birds. A pioneer in nature cinematography, his work has been shared by millions."

Thus begins *A Passion for Birds*, the story of John's career from his WWII experiences to his filming in Mexico and Central America.

John's interest in birds started in early childhood. The first birds he saw were a pair of long-tailed tits building a nest.

John related his fear during the war years that the Germans could, at any time, make him work in munitions factories. He went to Holland and when the Germans began taking young men from that country, he escaped to the south of France until the Allies came.

He discussed the Oriole Society and a priest who taught him how to band birds. As he learned more about the birds, he grew interested in their migration habits. He followed them. For most of his career, the birds determined his schedule and his journeys.

When John lived in the north, he went south for filming ventures. When he moved to the south, he traveled north every spring. The film showed repeated sequences of John either kneeling in marshes or standing in Arctic waters.

It gave an overview of John's many expeditions allowing viewers to see his work in diverse habitats and to follow his ever-expanding knowledge of birds. John traveled to the Arctic, the Netherlands Antilles, Ecuador, Costa Rica, Mexico and Brazil, following the migrations of North American birds.

Most of all, the film offered a glimpse of John's lifelong passion for his work.

Much of the film tracked John's search for hummingbirds. Viewers saw him with hummingbird feeders outside his trailer. John said he learned by being quiet and if he approached very slowly, he could get close to the birds. With a camera filming him inside his trailer, viewers saw the hummingbird feeder inside the trailer with no visitors. As he worked, the hummingbirds began to appear until a steady stream flew in and out of the door. He observed that every species he filmed there visited him inside his trailer.

In Bonaire, he found eleven Ruby-topaz hummingbird nests. It's the only place he ever found them. He learned how the male offers no help with domestic nesting chores but chooses to preen in nearby locations.

John's special affinity for the birds allowed him to capture spectacular close up interaction. The film showed close-up encounters with hummingbirds and a semipalmated plover. In Bonaire, John fed a hummingbird from a spoon. The film showed him carrying brown pelicans into the water to teach them to feed themselves.

In one scene John picked mosquitoes out of his coffee. As he stood in cold water, the hypothermia stiffened his muscles and joints. He found rattlesnakes, gila monsters and llamas. He climbed mountains and carried his equipment with him. In Mexico, he traveled with a guide and a pack mule.

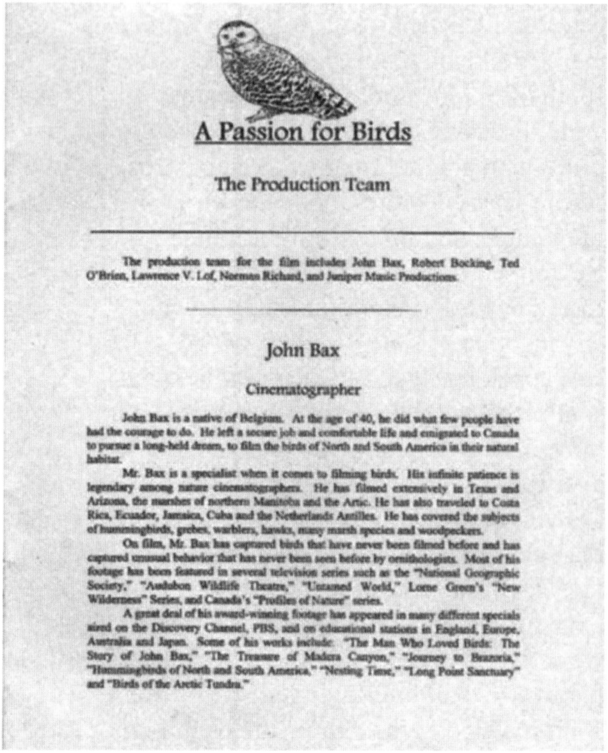

A Passion for Birds

The Production Team

The production team for the film includes John Bax, Robert Bocking, Ted O'Brien, Lawrence V. Lof, Norman Richard, and Juniper Music Productions.

John Bax

Cinematographer

John Bax is a native of Belgium. At the age of 40, he did what few people have had the courage to do. He left a secure job and comfortable life and emigrated to Canada to pursue a long-held dream, to film the birds of North and South America in their natural habitat.

Mr. Bax is a specialist when it comes to filming birds. His infinite patience is legendary among nature cinematographers. He has filmed extensively in Texas and Arizona, the marshes of northern Manitoba and the Artic. He has also traveled to Costa Rica, Ecuador, Jamaica, Cuba and the Netherlands Antilles. He has covered the subjects of hummingbirds, grebes, warblers, hawks, many marsh species and woodpeckers.

On film, Mr. Bax has captured birds that have never been filmed before and has captured unusual behavior that has never been seen before by ornithologists. Most of his footage has been featured in several television series such as the "National Geographic Society," "Audubon Wildlife Theatre," "Untamed World," Lorne Green's "New Wilderness" Series, and Canada's "Profiles of Nature" series.

A great deal of his award-winning footage has appeared in many different specials aired on the Discovery Channel, PBS, and on educational stations in England, Europe, Australia and Japan. Some of his works include: "The Man Who Loved Birds: The Story of John Bax," "The Treasure of Madera Canyon," "Journey to Brazoria," "Hummingbirds of North and South America," "Nesting Time," "Long Point Sanctuary" and "Birds of the Arctic Tundra."

A Passion for Birds Flyer

John commented on his filmmaking, "It makes me feel good… keeps me going. It's very important to do what you like to do."

The film ended with this comment about John:

"A gifted naturalist, a true artist, and more than almost anyone else, John Bax has taught us and brought to us the glorious beauty of nature.

Some of the birds in the film:

Holland:
- Black Woodpecker
- Crested Tit
- Great-crested Grebe

Green Finch
Noble Lapwing

Canada:
Arctic Loon
Baltimore Oriole
Cedar Waxwing
Horned Grebe
Jaeger
Northern Cardinal
Pie-billed Grebe
Red-necked Grebe
Sandhill Crane
Snow Goose
Vermillion Flycatcher
Western Grebe
Willow Ptarmigan

United States:
Brown Pelican
Green Parakeet
Least Grebe
Magnolia Warbler
Red-crowned Parrot
White Pelican
Whooping Crane
Yellow Warbler
Yellow-crowned Parrot

Netherlands Antilles, Mexico and Central America:
Black-tailed Train Bearer
Black-winged Stilt
Brown Pelican
Bumblebee Hummingbird
Canada Warbler
Greater Flamingo
Long-billed Scarborough
Macaw
Magnolia Warbler
Ruby-topaz Hummingbird
Sparkling Violet Ear
Sword-billed Hummingbird
Volcano Hummingbird

White Pelican
Whooping Crane

John's DVD Series

From 2000 to 2011, John produced a series of DVDs to continue his work. He and Alice traveled to Canada, Arizona, and throughout Texas.

When the 16mm camera and equipment became too heavy for John to use, he sold it to Larry Lof. He desperately missed filming. When he learned about video, he bought a Canon video camera and restarted his career.

He frequently asked Seth Patterson and Sandesh Kadur to edit the film for him – which they did, pro bono, in their spare time. Seth said John's work was easy to edit because he already had a story line in his mind. With many people, organization is the hardest job.

Seth loaned him an editing machine from the Gorgas Science Foundation. It was old and difficult to use. John taught himself. "He fussed with it night after night," Alice said.

One night in the middle of the night, Alice woke up and found John at the machine.

"I think I finally got it." John could hardly contain his excitement.

"You know Seth and Sandesh tell you if would be easier with a computer," Alice replied.

He used the video camera until the Gorgas Science Foundation bought a digital camera and computer for him.

John told Larry that he would continue to film hummingbirds if they provided a better camera. A couple of weeks later, John received a phone call. When he hung up the phone, he told Alice:

"Oh my word, what have I done? They are going to get me a camera and a computer."

Seth set up the digital equipment. John learned, with Seth's help, how to use it. At this time he was in his early eighties.

John focused on education and conservation in his films. He spent time explaining where to look for various species, and talked about their specific behaviors.

Although they lack the "professional production" feel of his previous work, they contain beautiful filming and John's love of studying birds is ever evident.

Films featured shorebirds, raptors and nature, many focusing on the Rio Grande Valley. His films are available at the island bookstore, Paragraphs on Padre Blvd.

One of his filming trips to Canada resulted in the following DVD.

Waterhen, Manitoba

Waterhen is located on the Waterhen River that flows into Manitoba Lake. John takes the viewer on a river journey as the film opens. He and Alice are in his canoe. He is looking for Western Grebes.

John finds many birds and explains their unique behaviors as the film captures their nests and activities. He finds a Phalarope nest where the male does all the incubating and raising of the young. The female lays the eggs, normally four, and then she is finished.

He filmed an American Avocet performing a "broken wing act." The bird has a nest with four eggs and lures danger away from the nest with this act. Several sequences involve ravens looking for eggs from a grebe's nest. In one, the raven successfully stole the eggs of a Red-necked Grebe.

The film includes a fox family – a mother with five babies. John captured some great shots of the kits that were curious about the camera.

John films a pair of Western Grebes covering their nest with moss. He loved their dance and showed quite a bit of footage of the grebes in action.

He found American Bitterns, Yellow Warblers, and Rails. The Rails make a dome over their nest. John tells the viewer to look for the dome in identifying the bird. Rails don't fly onto their nests — they run. John caught the nest landing several times.

John ends the film with shots of several orchid species found in the area.

"In my own way I like to preserve those rare moments that people have never gotten the opportunity to see. My effort is not as great as some I have seen who are trying so very hard to preserve what wildlife and beauty still exists." John Bax

Appendices

Appendix I: Filming Expeditions 1975–1997

Year	Location	Length of Time
1975	NW Territories, Canada	4 months
1978	Central Manitoba, Canada	6 weeks
1979	Central Manitoba, Canada	11 weeks
1981/82	Costa Rica, Central America	10 months
1982/83	Ecuador, South America	6 months
1984	Bonaire, Netherland Antilles	3 months
1985	Province of Ontario, Canada	3 months
1987	Seney NWR Upper Michigan	1 month
1988	Rio Grande Valley, Texas	1 year
1989	Madera Canyon, Arizona	3.5 months
1990	Brazoria NWR, Texas	3.5 months
1991	El Cielito, Mexico	5 months
1991/92	Brazil	3 months
1992	El Cielo, Mexico	4 months
1993	Texas	1 year
1994	Texas	1 year
1995	Belgium	1 month
1997	Jamaica & Cuba	2 months

Appendix II: Film List

Nesting Time-16mm, 1969-1971

A lot of patience and trust between the photographer and his subjects went into the making of this close-up glimpse into the lives and nests of many southern Ontario birds including the woodpecker, cedar waxwing and killdeer.

Long Point Sanctuary-16mm & video

Rare marsh birds hardly seen by the human visitor are in this telephoto view. Scenes include a bittern feeding its young and an extraordinary raid on a nest by a fox snake.

Birds & Animals Around the Great Lakes-16mm

It took three years to compile this unique collection of wildness in his own backyard. From the familiar to the seldom seen...including red fox, groundhog, yellow warbler, red-tailed hawk, great-horned owl, green heron, Tundra swan, turtle and albino mink.

North of the Treeline-16mm

A film record of a 3-month adventure along the western rim of Hudson Bay, where John Bax photographed 200,000 snow geese nesting on the Arctic tundra, the sights and sounds of the red-throated loon and the migration of Canada's largest caribou herd.

The Scientist & the Snowgeese-16mm

As a scientific expedition from the University of Western Ontario studied the geese of the North West Territories, the camera eavesdropped on the action, along with beautiful color close-ups of willow ptarmigan, snow bunting, Lapland longspurs and eider ducks.

Birds of the Arctic Tundra-16mm & video, 1984

Enjoy the nesting behavior of the red-throated and arctic loons in northern Canada.

Hummingbirds of North & South America-16mm & video

A four-year study on these beautiful and lovely creatures.

Warblers-16mm & video

Baby Animals (Disney production) – 16 mm

The Man who Loved Birds-16mm & video, 1986

The Treasure of Madera Canyon-16mm & video, 1989

Journey to Brazoria-16mm & video, 1990

At a Bend in a Mexican River-16mm & video, 1992

El Cielo: Forest in the Clouds-16mm & video, 1993

Treasures of the Rio Grande Delta-16mm & video, 1994

A Passion for Birds, 1996

DVD Productions

Lower Rio Grande Valley, 2009

Birds of the Rio Grande Valley, 2010

Backyard Treasures, 2010

Springtime in the Rio Grande Valley, 2010

Shorebirds & Raptors, 2010

Treasures of Deep South Texas Vol 1 & 2, 2011

All of John's raw 16mm film has been donated to the Macaulay Library at Cornell University Laboratory of Ornithology in Ithaca, New York. They plan to digitize the complete library of his work

Footage from much of the above-listed films has been used in documentaries including Untamed World, Disney, the Discovery Channel, PBS, Audubon Wildlife Theater, Profiles of Nature and Wildlife Cinema.

Cornell - John's 16mm raw films

Cornell - John's notes

The Macaulay Library is the world's leading scientific collection of biodiversity media, with more than 175,000 audio and 60,000 video recordings documenting the behavioral diversity of birds and other animals.

The Cornell Lab of Ornithology is a world leader in the study, appreciation, and conservation of birds... Founded in 1915, the Cornell Lab is a nonprofit organization supported by 45,000 friends and members. Our vibrant community includes 200,000 citizen-science participants from all walks of life and 5 million bird enthusiasts of all ages who connect with us online at All About Birds.

Appendix III: John Bax's Life List

English List - Alphabetized

Abert's Towhee
Acorn Woodpecker
Adorable Coquette (aka White-crested Coquette)
Allen's Hummingbird
Allied Emerald Hummingbird
Altamira Oriole
Amazon Kingfisher
American Avocet
American Bittern
American Coot
American Golden-Plover
American Goldfinch
American Kestrel
American Redstart
American Robin
American White Pelican
American Wigeon
American Woodcock
Andean Hillstar Hummingbird
Anhinga
Anna's Hummingbird
Arctic Loon
Arctic Tern
Arizona Woodpecker
Ash-throated Flycatcher
Audubon's Warbler
Azara's Spinetail
Azure Jay
Azure-crowned Hummingbird
Baird's Sandpiper
Bald Eagle
Baltimore Oriole (Northern)
Band-tailed Pigeon
Barn Owl
Barred Antshrike
Barrow's Goldeneye
Bay-breasted Warbler
Bay-headed Tanager
Bee Hummingbird
Belted Kingfisher
Berlepsch's Pigeon
Bewick's Wren
Black Phoebe
Black Seedeater *
Black Skimmer
Black Vulture
Black Woodpecker
Black-and-white Warbler
Black-backed Woodpecker
Black-bellied Plover
Black-bellied Whistling Duck
Black-billed Cuckoo
Blackburnian Warbler
Black-chinned Hummingbird
Black-crested Titmouse
Black-crowned Night Heron
Black-headed Grosbeak
Black-headed Oriole
Black-necked Stilt
Blackpoll Warbler
Black-tailed Trainbearer Hummingbird
Black-thighed Grosbeak
Black-throated Gray Warbler
Black-throated Green Warbler
Black-throated Sparrow
Black-winged Stilt
Blue Dacnis
Blue Grosbeak
Blue Jay
Blue Tanager
Blue-black Grosbeak
Blue-crowned Motmot
Blue-gray Gnatcatcher
Blue-throated Hummingbird
Blue-throated Toucanet

Blue-winged Teal
Blue-winged Warbler
Boat-billed Flycatcher
Boat-tailed Grackle
Bobolink
Bobwhite Quail
Bohemian Waxwing
Bonaparte's Gull
Brazilian Great Black Hawk
Brewer's Blackbird
Bronzy Hermit Hummingbird
Bridled Titmouse
Broad-billed Hummingbird
Broad-tailed Hummingbird
Broad-winged Hawk
Bronzed Cowbird
Bronze-winged Woodpecker
Brown Creeper
Brown Jay
Brown Pelican
Brown Thrasher
Brown Towhee
Brown-crested Flycatcher
Brown-headed Cowbird
Brown-headed Nuthatch
Buff-bellied Hummingbird
Buff-breasted Sandpiper
Buff-collared Nightjar
Bufflehead
Buff-throated Saltator
Bumblebee Hummingbird
Cabanis's Ground Sparrow
Cactus Wren
Calliope Hummingbird
Canada Goose
Canada Warbler
Canvasback
Canvasback Duck
Canyon Wren
Cape May Warbler
Carolina Chickadee
Carolina Wren
Caspian Tern
Cassin's Dove
Cattle Egret
Cave Swallow
Cayenne Squirrel Cuckoo
Cayenne Wood Rail
Cedar Waxwing
Chestnut-sided Warbler
Chimney Swift
Chipping Sparrow
Cinnamon Teal
Clapper Rail
Cliff Swallow
Coal Black Flowerpiercer
Collared Aracari
Collared Trogon
Common Black Hawk
Common Bushtit
Common Crow
Common Egret
Common Grackle
Common Loon
Common Moorhen
Common Murre
Common Nighthawk
Common Potoo
Common Raven
Common Yellowthroat
Cooper's Hawk
Costa Rican Manakin
Costa's Hummingbird
Crested Caracara
Crested Tit
Crissal Thrasher
Cuban Emerald Hummingbird
Curve-billed Thrasher
Delattre Warbler
Derby Flycatcher
Dickcissel
Double-crested Cormorant
Downy Woodpecker
Dusky-capped Flycatcher
Eared Grebe
Eastern Bluebird
Eastern Kingbird
Eastern Meadowlark

Eastern Phoebe
Eastern Screech Owl
Eastern Wood-pewee
Elegant Trogon (aka Coppery-tailed Trogon)
Elf Owl
Elicia's Hummingbird
Evening Grosbeak
Ferruginous Pygmy-owl
Field Sparrow
Flamulated Owl
Fork-tailed Emerald Hummingbird
Forster's Tern
Frantzius' Aracari
Fulvous Whistling Duck
Gadwall
Gambel's Quail
Gartered (Violaceus) Trogon
Giant Hummingbird
Gila Woodpecker
Giraud's Flycatcher
Glaucous Gull
Golden-crowned Kinglet
Golden-fronted Woodpecker
Golden-masked Tanager
Golden-winged Warbler
Gray Catbird
Gray Flycatcher
Gray Jay
Gray Vireo
Gray's Robin
Gray-breasted Martin
Gray-breasted Wood-wren
Gray-cheeked Thrush
Gray-crowned Yellowthroat
Great Blue Heron
Great Gray Owl
Great Horned Owl
Great Sapphirewing Hummingbird
Great Thrush
Great-crested Flycatcher
Greater Roadrunner
Greater Roadrunner
Greater Yellowlegs
Great-tailed Grackle
Green Hermit
Green Heron
Green Honeycreeper
Green Jay
Green Kingfisher
Green Violet-ear Hummingbird
Green-tailed Trainbearer Hummingbird
Green-winged Teal
Guatemalan Quetzal
Gull-billed Tern
Hairy Woodpecker
Harris's Hawk
Harris's Sparrow
Henslow's Sparrow
Hepatic Tanager
Hermit Thrush
Hermit Warbler
Hicks' Seedeater
Hoffman's Woodpecker
Hooded Merganser
Hooded Oriole
Hooded Warbler
Horned Lark
House Finch
Hudsonian Godwit
Inca Dove
Indigo Bunting
Jalapa Trogon
Jamaican Mango Hummingbird
Keel-billed Toucan
Killdeer
King Eider
King Rail
Ladder Backed Woodpecker
Lande's Manakin
Lapland Longspur
Lark Bunting
Lark Sparrow
Laughing Gull
Lazuli Bunting
Le Conte's Sparrow
Least Bittern
Least Flycatcher

Least Grebe
Least Sandpiper
Least Tern
Lesser Goldfinch
Lesser Goldfinch
Lesser Scaup
Lesser Violet Ear
Lesser Yellowlegs
Lesson's Motmot
Lincoln's Sparrow
Lineated Woodpecker
Little Blue Heron
Little Group Dove *
Little Hermit Hummingbird
Loggerhead Shrike
Long-billed Curlew
Long-billed Dowitcher
Long-billed Marsh Wren
Long-billed Starthroat Hummingbird
Long-tailed (Silky Flycatcher) Ptilogony
Long-tailed Jaeger
Lousiana Waterthrush
Lucifer Hummingbird
Lucy's Warbler
Magnificent Hummingbird
Magnolia Warbler
Mangrove Warbler
Marbled Godwit
Masked Duck
Masked Tityra
Massena Trogon (Slaty-tailed)
Mexican Bananaquit
Mexican Jay
Mexican Junco
Minor Frigatebird
Mottled Duck
Mountain Chickadee
Mountain Plover
Mountain Velvetbreast Hummingbird
Mourning Dove
Mourning Warbler
Nashville Warbler
Northern Beardless Tyrannulet
Northern Cardinal
Northern Gannet
Northern Goshawk
Northern Parula Warbler
Northern Waterthrush
Olive Grasquit
Orange-billed Nightingale-Thrush
Orange-billed Sparrow
Orange-crowned Warbler
Orchard Oriole
Oregon Junco
Osprey
Ovenbird
Pacific Rail
Palm Tanager
Palm Warbler
Parasitic Jaeger
Pectoral Sandpiper
Phainopepla
Philadelphia Vireo
Pied-billed Grebe
Pileated Woodpecker
Pine Siskin
Piping Plover
Plain Chachalaca
Plush Tanager *
Prairie Warbler
Prothonotary Warbler
Purple Martin
Purple Sandpiper
Purple-throated Fruitcrow
Purple-throated Mountain Gem Hummingbird
Pygmy Nuthatch
Pyrrhuloxia
Rainbow Starfrontlet Hummingbird
Red Phalarope
Red-bellied Woodpecker
Red-billed Pigeon
Red-breasted Merganser
Red-breasted Nuthatch
Reddish Egret
Red-eared Parrot *
Red-eyed Vireo
Red-faced Warbler

Redhead Duck
Red-headed Woodpecker
Red-necked Grebe
Red-necked Phalarope
Red-shafted Flicker
Red-tailed Hawk
Red-throated Loon
Red-winged Blackbird
Richmond Sparrow
Ring-billed Gull
Ringed Kingfisher
Ring-necked Duck
Rock Pigeon
Rock Ptarmigan
Rock Wren
Rocky Mountain Rail *
Roseate Spoonbill
Rose-breasted Grosbeak
Ross' Goose
Rough-legged Hawk
Rough-winged Swallow
Ruby-crowned Kinglet
Ruby-throated Hummingbird
Rucker's Hermit
Ruddy Ground Dove
Ruffed Grouse
Rufous Hummingbird
Rufous-collared Sparrow
Rufous-crowned Sparrow
Rufous-sided Towhee
Rufous-tailed Hummingbird
Rusty Blackbird
Sabine's Gull
Sage Thrasher
Sandhill Crane
Sapphire-vented Puffleg
Savannah Sparrow
Saw-whet Owl
Say's Phoebe
Scaled Pigeon
Scaled Quail
Scarlet Tanager
Scarlet-bellied Mountain Tanager
Scissor-tailed Flycatcher
Scott's Oriole
Sedge Wren
Semi-palmated Plover
Semi-palmated Sandpiper
Sharp-shinned Hawk
Sharp-tailed Grouse
Sharp-tailed Sparrow
Shining Sunbeam Hummingbird
Short-billed Dowitcher
Silver-throated Jay
Silver-throated Tanager
Simon's Hummingbird *
Slate-colored Junco
Smooth-billed Ani
Snow Bunting
Snow Goose
Snowy Egret
Snowy-breasted Hummingbird
Solitary Sandpiper
Solitary Vireo
Song Sparrow
Sooty Robin
Sora
Southern House Wren
Sparkling Violet-ear Hummingbird
Spot-breasted Oriole
Spotted Sandpiper
Spruce Grouse
Steller's Jay
Stilt Sandpiper
Streaked Saltator
Sulphur-bellied Flycatcher
Sumichrast's Blackbird
Summer Tanager
Surf Scoter
Swainson's Thrush
Swallow-tailed Kite
Swamp Sparrow
Sword-billed Hummingbird
Tawny Antpitta
Tennessee Warbler
Thayer's Gull
Thick-billed Seedeater
Three-toed Woodpecker

Townsend's Warbler
Tree Sparrow
Tree Swallow
Tri-colored Heron
Tropical Kingbird
Tundra Swan
Turkey Vulture
Tyrian Metaltail Hummingbird
Upland Plover (Sandpiper)
Varied Thrush
Veery
Velvet Manakin
Verdin
Vermillion Flycatcher
Violet Sabrewing
Violet-crowned Hummingbird
Violet-green Swallow
Virginia Rail
Wagler's Oropendola
Warbling Vireo
Water Pipit
Western Flycatcher
Western Grebe
Western Kingbird
Western Meadowlark
Western Screech Owl
Western Scrub Jay
Western Streamertail Hummingbird
Western Tanager
Western Wood Pewee
Whip-poor-will
Whiskered Screech Owl
White Ibis
White-breasted Nuthatch
White-breasted Wood Wren
White-crowned Sparrow
White-eyed Vireo
White-faced Ibis
White-rumped Sandpiper
White-tailed Emerald Hummingbird
White-tailed Kite
White-throated Magpie
White-throated Mountain-gem
White-throated Robin
White-throated Sparrow
White-throated Swift
White-tipped Jay
White-tipped Tody Flycatcher
White-winged Dove
White-winged Scoter
White-winged Tanager
Wild Turkey
Willet
Willow Ptarmigan
Wilson's Phalarope
Wilson's Plover
Wilson's Warbler
Wood Duck
Wood Stork
Wood Thrush
Worm-eating Warbler
Yellow Rail
Yellow-bellied Elaenia
Yellow-bellied Flycatcher
Yellow-bellied Redstart (Slate-throated)
Yellow-bellied Sapsucker
Yellow-breasted Chat
Yellow-headed Blackbird
Yellow-rumped Warbler
Yellow-shafted Flicker
Yellow-throated Atlapetes
Yellow-throated Vireo
Yellow-throated Warbler

* Author's Note: Denotes bird species I could not verify. I don't know if I misread John's writing, he spelled words wrong or used an uncommon name.

Belgische Lijst-Alfabetisch

Aalscholver	Phalacrocorax carbo	Great Cormorant
Appelvink	Coccothraustes coccothraustes	Hawfinch
Baardmees	Panurus biarnicus	Bearded Tit
Barmsijs	Carduelis cabaret	Common Redpoll
Bergeend	Tadorna tadorna	Common Shelduck
Blauwe Kiekendief	Circus cyaneus	Hen Harrier
Blauwe Reiger	Ardea cinerea	Grey Heron
Boerenzwaluw	Hirundo rustica	Barn Swallow
Bokje	Lymnocryptes minimus	Jack Snipe
Bontbekplevier	Charadrius hiaticula	Great Ringed Plover
Bonte Kraai	Corvus cornix	Hooded Crow
Bonte strandloper	Calidris alpina	Dunlin
Bonte Vliegenvanger	Ficedula hypoleuca	Pied Flycatcher
Boomklever	Sitta europaea	Wood Nuthatch
Boomkruiper	Certhia brachydactyla	Short Toed Treecreeper
Boomleeuwerik	Lullula arborea-	Wood Lark
Boompieper	Anthus trivialis	Tree Pipit
Boomvalk	Falco subbuteo	Hobby
Bosrietzanger	Acrocephalus palustris	March Warbler
Bosruiter	Tringa glareola	Wood Sandpiper
Bosuil	Strix aluco	Tawny Owl
Braamsluiper	Sylvia currica	Lesser Whitethroat
Brandgans	Branta leucopsis	Barnacle Goose
Brilduiker	Bucephala clangula	Common Goldeneye
Bruine Kiekendief	Circus aeruginosus	March Harrier
Buizerd	Buteo buteo	Common Buzzard
Canadagans	Branta canadensis	Canada Goose
Dodaars	Podiceps rufficolis	Little Grebe
Draaihals	Jynx torquila	Wryneck
Drieteenmeeuw	Rissa tridactyla	Kiitiwake
Drieteenstrandloper	Calidris alba	Sanderling
Duinpieper	Anthus campestris	Tawny Pipit
Dwergooruil	Otus scops	Eurasian Scops-Owl
Dwergstern	Sterna albifrons	Little Tern
Eidereend	Sometaria mollissima	Common Eider
Ekster	Pica pica	Magpie
Europese kanarie	Serinus serinus	European Serin
Fazant	Phasianus colchicus	Common Pheasant
Fitis	Philloscopus trochilus	Willow Warbler
Fluiter	Philloscopus sibilatrix	Wood Warbler
Fuut	Podiceps cristatus	Great Crested Grebe
Geelgors	Emberiza citrinella	Yellow Hammer
Gekraagde Roodstaart	Phoenicurus phoenicurus	Common Redstart

Gele Kwikstaart	Motacilla flava	Yellow Wagtail
Geoorde Fuut	Podiceps nigricollis	Black Necked Grebe
Gierzwaluw	Apus apus	Common Swift
Glanskopmees	Parus palustris	March Tit
Goudhaantje	Regulus regulus	Goldcrest
Goudplevier	Pluvialis apricaria	European Golden Plover
Grauwe kiekendief	Circus pygargus	Montagu's Harrier
Goudvink	Pyrrhula pyrrhula	Bullfinch
Graspieper	Anthus pratensis	Meadow Pipit
Grasmus	Sylvia communis	Common Whitethroat
Grauwe gans	Anser anser	Greylag Goose
Grauwe gors	Miliaria calandra	Corn Bunting
Grauwe klauwier	Lanius collurio	Red-Bached Shrike
Grauwe Vliegenvanger	Muscicapa striata	Spotted Flycatcher
Groenvink	Chloris chloris	Greenfinch-
Groenpootruiter	Tringa nebularia	Common Greenshank
Groene Specht	Picus veridis	Green Woodpecker
Grote bonte specht	Dendrocopus major	Great Spotted Woodpecker
Grote Gele Kwikstaart	Motacilla cinerea	Grey Wagtail
Grote Karekiet	Acrocephalus arundinaceus	Great Reed Warbler
Grote Lijster	Turdus viscivorus	Mistle Thrush
Grote Stern	Sterna sandvicensis	Sandwich Tern
Grote Zaagbek	Mergus merganser	Goosander
Grote Zee-eend	Melanitta fusca	Velvet Scoter
Grutto	Limosa limosa	Black Tailed Godwit
Havik	Accipiter gentilis	Northern Goshawk
Heggemus	Prunella modularis	Hedge Accentor
Holenduif	Columba oenas	Stock Dove
Houtduif	Columba palumbus	Wood Pigeon
Houtsnip	Scolopax rusticola	Woodcock
Huismus	Passer domesticus	House Sparrow
Huiszwaluw	Delichon urbica	House Martin
Ijseend	Clangula hyemalis	Long-Tailed Duck
Ijsvogel	Alcedo atthis	Common Kingfisher
Kanoet Strandloper	Calidris canutus	Red Knot
Kauw	Corvus monedula	Eurasian Jackdaw
Keep	Fringilla montifringilla	Brambling
Kemphaan	Philomachus pugnax	Ruff
Kerkuil	Tyto alba	Barn Owl
Kievit	Vanellus vanellus	Northern Lapwing
Klapekster	Lanius excubitor	Great Grey Shrike
Kleine Bonte Specht	Dendrocopos minor	Lesser Spotted Woodpecker
Kleine Karekiet	Acrocephalus scirpaceus	Red Warbler
Kleine Strandloper	Calidris minuta	Little Stint

Kleine Zwaan	Cygnus bewickie	Tundra Swan
KleinePlevier	Charadrius dubius	Little Ringed Plover
Kleinste Strandloper	Caladris minutila	Least Sandpiper
Kneu	Carduelis cannabina	Linet
Kluut	Recurvirostra avosetta	Avocet
Knobbel Zwaan	Cygnus olor	Mute Swan
Koekoek	Cuculus canorus	Common Cuckoo
Kokmeeuw	Larus ridibundus	Black Headed Gull
Kolgans	Anser albifrons	White Fronted Goose
Koolmees	Parus major	Great Tit
Koperwiek	Turdus iliacus	Redwing
Korhaan	Tetrao tetrix	Black Grouse
Kraanvogel	Grus grus	Common Crane
Krakeend	Anas stepera	Gadwall
Kramsvogel	Turdus pilaris	Fieldfare
Kruisbek	Loxia curvirostra	Crossbill
Kuifaalscholver	Stictocarbo aristoteles	Shag
Kuifduiker	Podiceps auritus	Slavonian Grebe
Kuifeend	Aythia fulicula	Tufted Duck
Kuifleeuwerik	Galerida cristata	Crested Lark
Kuifmees	Parus cristatus	Crested Tit
Kwartel	Coturnix coturnix	Common Quail
Kwartelkoning	Crex crex	Corn Crake
Staartmees	Aegithalos caudatus	Long Tailed Tit
Lepelaar	Platalea leucorodia	Eurasian Spoonbill
Mantelmeeuw	Larus marinus	Great Black-backed Gull
Matkopmees	Parus montanus	Willow Tit
Meerkoet	Fulica atra	Common Coot
Merel	Turdus merula	Blackbird
Middelste Zaagbek	Mergus serrator	Red Brested Merganser
Nachtegaal	Luscinia megarhynchos	Rufous Nightingale
Nachtwaluw	Caprimulgus europaeus	European Nightjar
Nonnetje	Mergus albellus	Smew
Notenkraker	Nucifraga caryocatactes	Nutcracker
Oehoe	Bubo bubo	Eagle Owl
Oeverloper	Actitis hypoleucos	Common Sandpiper
Oeverpieper	Anthus petrosus	Rockpipit
Oeverzwaluw	Riparia riparia	Sand Martin
Ooievaar	Cinonia ciconia	White Stork
Ortolaan	Emberiza hortulano	Ortolan Bunting
Paapje	Saxicola rubetra	Whinchat
Patrijs	Perdix perdix	Grey Partridge
Pijlstaarteend	Anas acuta	Northern Pintail
Porseleinhoen	Porzana porzana	Spotted Crake

Pimpelmees	Parus caeruleus	Blue Tit
Putter	Carduelis carduelis	Goldfinch
Ransuil	Asio otus	Long Eared Owl
Regenwulp	Numenius pheaopus	Whimbrel
Rietgans	Anser brachyrhynchus	Pink-footed Goose
Rietgors	Emberiza schoeniclus	Reed Bunting
Rietzanger	Acrocephalus schoenobaenus	Sedge Warbler
Ringmus	Passer montanus	Tree Sparrow
Rode wouw	Milvus milvus	Red Kite
Roek	Corvus frugilegus	Rook
Roerdomp	Botaurus stellaris	Great Bittern
Roodborst	Erithacus rubecula	Robin
Roodborsttapuit	Saxicola rubicola	Common Stonechet
Roodhalsfuut	Podiceps grisegena	Red-necked Grebe
Roodkeelduiker	Gavia stellata	Red-troated Diver
Rosse Grutto	Limosa laponica	Bar-tailed Godwit
Ruigpootuil	Aegolius funereus	Tengmalm's Owl
Rotgans	Branta bernicla	Dark Bellied Brent Goose
Ruigpootbuizerd	Buteo lagopus	Rough-Legged Buzzard
Scholekster	Haematopus ostralegus	Oystercatcher
Slechtvalk	Falco peregrinus	Peregrine
Slobeend	Anas clypeata	Northern Shoveler
Smelleken	Falco columbarius	Merlin
Smient	Anas penelope	Eurasian Wigeon
Sneeuwgors	Plectrophenax nivalis	Snow Bunting
Snor	Locustella luscinioides	Savi's Warbler
Sperwer	Accipiter nisus	Eurasian Sperrohawk
Spotvogel	Hippolais icterina	Icterine Warbler
Spreeuw	Sturnus vulgaris	Common Starling
Sprinkhaanrietzanger	Locustella naevia	Grasshopper Warbler
Steenloper	Arenaria interpres	Turnstone
Steenuil	Athene noctua	Little Owl
Steltkluut	Himantopus himantopus	Black Winged Stilt
Stormmeeuw	Larus canus	Common Gull
Strandplevier	Charadrius alexandrinus	Kentish Plover
Sijs	Carduelis spinus	Siskin
Tafeleend	Aythya ferina	Common Pochard
Tapuit	Oenanthe oenanthe	Northern Wheatear
Temminkstrandloper	Calidris temminckii	Temminck's Stint
Tjiftjaf	Philloscopus collybita	Chiffchaff
Toppereend	Aythya marila	Greater Scaup
Torenvalk	Falco tinnunculus	Common Kestrel
Tortelduif	Streptopelia turtur	Turtle Dove
Tuinfluiter	Sylvia borin	Garden Warbler

Tureluur	Tringa totanus	Common Redshank
Turkse Tortel	Streptopelia decaocto	Collared Dove
Veldleeuwerik	Aulauda arvensis	Sky Lark
Velduil	Asio flammeus	Short-eared Owl
Vink	Fringilla coelebs	Chaffinch
Visdief	Sterna hirundo	Common Tern
Vlaamse Gaai	Garrulus glandarius	Eurasian Jay
Vuurgoudhaantje	Regulus ignicapillus	Firecre
Waterral	Rallus aquaticus	Water Rail
Watersnip	Gallinago gallinago	Common Snipe
Waterspreeuw	Cinclus cinclus	Dipper
Waterhoen	Gallinula chloropus	Moorhen
Wespendief	Pernis apivorus	Honey Buzzard
Wielewaal	Oriolus oriolus	Golden Oriole
Wilde Eend	Anas platyrhynchos	Mallard
Wilde Zwaan	Cygnus cygnus	Whooper Swan
Winterkoning	Troglodytes troglodytes	Wren
Wintertaling	Anas crecca	Common Teal
Witgatje	Tringa ochropus	Green Sandpiper
Witoogeend	Aythya nyroca	Ferruginous Duck
Witgesterde blauwborst	Luscinia sveccica	Bluethroat
Witte Kwikstaart	Motacilla alba	Pied Wagtail
Wouwaap	Ixobrychus minutus	Little Bittern
Wulp	Numenius arquata	Curlew
Zanglijster	Turdus philomelos	Song Trush
Zilvermeeuw	Larus argentatus	Herring Gull
Zilverplevier	Pluvialis sqartarola	Grey Plover
Zomertaling	Anas querquedula	Garganey
Zwarte kraai	Corvus corone	Carrion Crow
Zwarte mees	Parus ater	Coal Tit
Zwarte Roodstaart	Phoenicurus ochruros	Black Redstart
Zwarte Ruiter	Tringa erytropus	Spoted Redshank
Zwarte Specht	Dryocopus martius	Black Woodpecker
Zwarte Stern	Chlidonias niger	Black Tern
Zwarte wouw	Milvus migrans	Black Kite
Zwarte Zee-eend	Melanitta nigra	Common Scoter
Zwartkop Grasmus	Sylvia atricapilla	Black Cap

Bibliography

Books

Anderson, C. LeRoy, Anderson, Joanne R. and Ohkura, Yunosuke, Editors. *No Longer Silent: World-Wide Memories of the Children of World War Two*. Pictorial Histories Publishing Co., Inc., Missoula, Montana, 1995.

Dunn, Jon L. and Alderfer, Jonathan. *National Geographic Field Guide to the Birds of North America, Fifth Edition*. National Geographic. 2006.

Lof, Lawrence and Patterson, Seth. *El Valle: The Rio Grande Delta*. Gorgas Science Foundation. Brownsville, Texas, 2010.

Michman, Dan, Editor. *Belgium and the Holocaust: Jews, Belgians, Germans*. Yad Vashem Publications. 1998.

Sibley, David Allen. *The Sibley Guide to Birds*. Knopf. 2000.

Films

A Passion for Birds: The Adventures of Nature Cinematographer John Bax. Gorgas Science Foundation, 1996.

At a Bend in a Mexican River. (VHS) Gorgas Science Foundation, Inc. Brownsville, TX. 1992

Birds of the Arctic Tundra., Profiles of Nature: Discovery Showcase. A KEG Production

El Cielo: Forest in the Clouds. Gorgas Science Foundation, Inc. Brownsville, TX. 1993.

Hummingbirds. Profiles of Nature: Discovery Showcase. A KEG Production

Journey to Brazoria.

The Man Who Loved Birds.

The Treasure of Madera Canyon: John Bax in Arizona. The KEG Productions in association with CFCN-TV Calgary, the Global Television Network, and The Family Channel.

The World of Baby Animals.

Treasures of the Rio Grande Delta.
Warblers. Profiles in Nature, A KEG Production.

DVDs:

Backyard Treasures. John & Alice Bax, South Padre Island Birding and Nature Center, 2009.
Birds of the Rio Grande Valley. John & Alice Bax. 2010.
Lower Rio Grande Valley Part 2, John & Alice Bax. 2009.
Shorebirds & Raptors. John Bax. South Padre Island Birding and Nature Center, 2009.
Springtime in the Rio Grande Valley. John & Alice Bax. South Padre Island Birding and Nature Center, 2009.
The Bruce Peninsula. John & Alice Bax.
Waterhen. John & Alice Bax. 2009.

Publications

Turnhout Public Relations Department Brochure

Personal Interviews

Bax, Alice. Multiple personal interviews
Bax, Emiel. Personal interview
Bax, John. Multiple personal interviews
Bax, John, Jr. Personal interview
Bax, Joseph. Personal interview
Bax, Leo. Personal interviews
Bax, Maureen. Email correspondence
Bocking, Bob. Email correspondence
Colley, Scarlet. Personal interview
Clock, Benjamin, Cornell Laboratory of Ornithology
Hindman, Glen. Personal interview
Kadur, Sandesh, Nature Cinematographer, Email correspondence
Lof, Lawrence (Larry), Personal Interview
Mercieca, Tony. Wildlife Photographer, Personal interview
Patterson, Seth. Nature Photographer, Personal interview
Peck, George K. Ornithologist, Email correspondence
Purcell, Bill. Birder. Email correspondence
Sandefur, Madeleine, Birder and Photographer, Email correspondence
Sinclair, Steve. Writer and Photographer, Personal interview

Zieger, Lee. Nature Photographer, Personal Interview

Resources

Cornell Laboratory of Ornithology, Ithaca, New York

Websites

www.allaboutbirds.org
http://www.antwerp-tourist-guide.com/
http://audubonportland.org/sanctuaries/wcc/stories/imprinting
www.azgfd.gov
http://www.backyardchirper.com/bird-info-117.html
http://www.backyardnature.net/birdprnt.htm
http://www.belgium.under.ground.freeservers.com/index.html
http://birdingsiteguide.com/index.php?option=com_content&task=view&id=25&Itemid=69http://www.birdnature.com
www.birds.cornell.edu
http://costa-rica-guide.com/parks/poas.htm http://www.desertmuseum.org/books/nhsd_phainopepla.php
www.desertusa.com
http://www.eagles.org/vu-study/behaviors/imprinting.php
www.galactic-guide.com/articles/6R40.html
http://www.gsfinc.org/focus/mexico/
http://www.history.com/this-day-in-history/belgium-surrenders uncon ditionally
http://www.historyorb.com/events/date/1925?p=2
http://www.historyplace.com/worldwar2/timeline/ww2time.htm
http://identify.whatbird.com/
www.imperial.edu
http://law2.umkc.edu/faculty/projects/ftrials/scopes/y1925.htm
http://www.lonelyplanet.com/maps/europe/belgium/
http://www.mendeley.com/research/gustavo-orces-fernando-ortiz-development-ornithology-ecuador/
http://mexicolesstraveled.com/elcielo.htm
http://www.neotropicalbirdclub.org/articles/24/Venturini.pdf
http://noviomagus.tripod.com/background-history.htm
http://onlinelibrary.wiley.com/doi/10.1046/j.1474-919X.2002.00053_3.x/pdf
http://www.mexicotravelvacations.com/article/492/Mexican-Animal-

Life-Snakes-Mexico-vacation-help/
http://www.planeta.com/ecotravel/mexico/tamaulipas/elcielo.html
http://www.planetware.com/belgium/turnhout-b-a-th.htm
http://www.squidoo.com/dangerous-snakes-of-latin-america
http://www.teacheroz.com/WWIImaps.htm
http://www.thegoosesmother.com/id6.html
http://www.thepeoplehistory.com/1925.html
http://www.trabel.com/antwerp.htm
http://vaxxine.com/mgdsite/year/1925.htm
http://www.weatheronline.co.uk/reports/climate/Belgium.htm
http://en.wikipedia.org/wiki/1965_in_Canada
http://www.worldatlas.com/webimage/countrys/europe/be.htm
http://www.worldatlas.com/webimage/countrys/europe/lgcolor/becolor.htm